**Books are to be returned on or before
the last date below.**

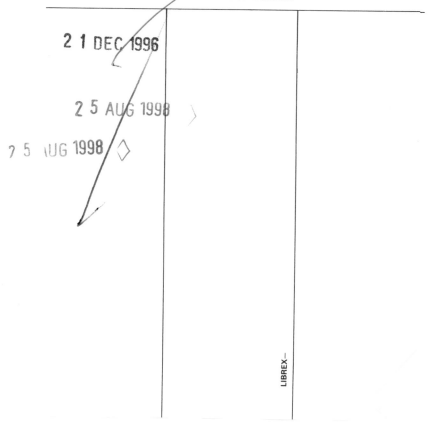

2 1 DEC 1996

2 5 AUG 1998

2 5 AUG 1998

LIBREX–

SUSTAINABLE SEWERAGE

SUSTAINABLE SEWERAGE

Guidelines for community schemes

R. A. REED

INTERMEDIATE TECHNOLOGY PUBLICATIONS
in association with the
WATER, ENGINEERING AND DEVELOPMENT CENTRE
1995

Intermediate Technology Publications
103-105 Southampton Row, London WC1B 4HH, UK

© Water, Engineering and Development Centre 1995

A CIP record for this book is available from
the British Library

ISBN Paperback 1 85339 305 3

Typeset by Karen Betts
Designed by Rod Shaw

Printed by SRP, Exeter

CONTENTS

Tables

Figures

Photographs

ACKNOWLEDGEMENTS

The author wishes to acknowledge the assistance given by the Engineering Division of the British Overseas Development Administration in funding the research from which much of the information found in this book derives.

He would also like to express his thanks to the following people for their assistance in the preparation of this book.

Prof. J.A. Pickford, Emeritus Professor Water and Waste Engineering for Developing Countries, Loughborough University of Technology, UK.

Mr I. K. Smout, Programme Manager, Water, Engineering and Development Centre, Loughborough University of Technology, UK.

Prof. H. Tebbutt, Director, Group Research, Biwater Ltd, UK.

Mr M. Vines, Research Assistant (formerly), Water, Engineering and Development Centre, Loughborough University of Technology, UK.

INTRODUCTION

This book is about sewers on domestic properties and in the communal or upper sections of the sewer network. This area contains the greater part of a sewerage network and is where most savings and changes can be made. It is also the area of most concern to the users. Most texts on the subject separate house sewerage from communal sewerage because they are the responsibility of different groups. This book promotes their consideration together. Sustainable sewerage in poor countries is viable only if communities are able to repay much of the capital investment and, as far as property owners are concerned, this means the on-plot costs as well as the communal costs. It is only by considering the two together that total costs can be minimized. Trunk sewers (see Glossary of terms, Appendix 1) are generally ignored because there are few changes that can be made to current technologies and practices. Wastewater treatment is completely ignored. From an environmental viewpoint, treatment is undoubtedly important, but it is expensive, and most of the communities at which this book is aimed would consider it a much lower priority than sewerage. Ample literature is available describing conventional and low-cost wastewater treatment processes, and the interested reader is recommended to consult one of those textbooks.

As far as possible the book follows the stages involved in the design, construction, operation and maintenance of a sewerage scheme.

Chapter 1 gives the background on why sewerage might be considered necessary by a community and explains the constraints on its installation.

Chapter 2 suggests a methodology for selecting the communities that should have priority for the provision of sewerage. The method is based on an objective evaluation of measurable criteria. The aim is to minimize the amount of subjective decision-making involved in the selection procedure.

Chapter 3 is provided for the benefit of readers who are unaware of how sewerage schemes are normally designed. A knowledge of the conventional approach to sewerage design is important for a full understanding of the implications of the changes proposed in this book.

Chapter 4 examines the ways of minimizing the cost of constructing new sewerage schemes. Not only does the chapter suggest changes in the design parameters, it also describes ways of reducing the cost of individual components and economizing on construction management costs.

Chapter 5 discusses one of the biggest problems with existing schemes, that of poor connection rates. If people do not connect to a sewer they will not benefit from it. In addition the sewers may not function correctly because of low flow rates and the implementing agency will have little chance of recouping its investment. The chapter looks at why people do not connect, and suggests ways of encouraging them to do so.

Chapter 6 tackles the problems of poor operation and maintenance. Ways are suggested of keeping operation and maintenance costs to a minimum and alternative implementation options are described.

Chapter 7 concentrates on money. It examines ways of keeping tariff collection charges to a minimum whilst ensuring that the tariff is efficiently collected.

Chapter 8 describes how the measures discussed in Chapters 4 to 7 can be combined. Three examples of combining these measures are described in detail: simplified sewerage, condominial sewerage and sewered interceptor tank systems.

Appendix 1 provides a glossary of terms.

Appendix 2 gives design details for the construction of interceptor tanks.

CHAPTER 1
Background

THE MOVEMENT OF populations to the towns has increased dramatically in developing countries in recent decades. Many of these new immigrants live on the edges of the cities, often illegally squatting on marginal land. The provision of basic infrastructure for such communities is a major cause of concern for many municipal corporations.

Failure to provide services such as sanitation leads to an increase in disease and social unrest, and unfortunately the immigrants are generally poor and unable to pay for the services they require. At the same time the financial resources of city governments are fully extended trying to maintain existing services; any spare resources a municipality may have are more likely to be used for providing facilities in the more affluent communities than in slum areas. Generally, the rich have political influence and the resources to contribute to or to repay investments.

The layout of low-income urban housing areas tends to change with time. Initially housing density is low and properties are clustered round the area entry points. Gradually housing density increases and the built-up area extends. The changes in settlement are often mirrored by changes in income levels. The residents of new settlements tend to be poor, but as the settlements become established, income and education levels rise, fuelling the demand for better services.

One of the most basic services is sanitation, particularly the disposal of human faeces and urine (excreta). Sanitation is usually considered to include the disposal of excreta, liquids from domestic and personal activities (sullage), and solid waste (refuse or garbage).

In the early stages of a settlement's development, housing density tends to be low, as does per capita water consumption. At this stage the most appropriate form of excreta disposal is usually some form of on-site sanitation system, such as a pit latrine.

Further increases in housing density, water consumption and family income will eventually lead to claims by the community that their on-site sanitation systems are no longer satisfactory. Unfortunately the only realistic alternative is sewerage (the removal of human excreta and domestic liquid wastes using buried pipelines) which, as will be seen later, is far more expensive to construct and maintain than on-site systems. It is paramount therefore that any plans to install sewerage must first of all determine whether on-site systems have, in fact, already failed.

1

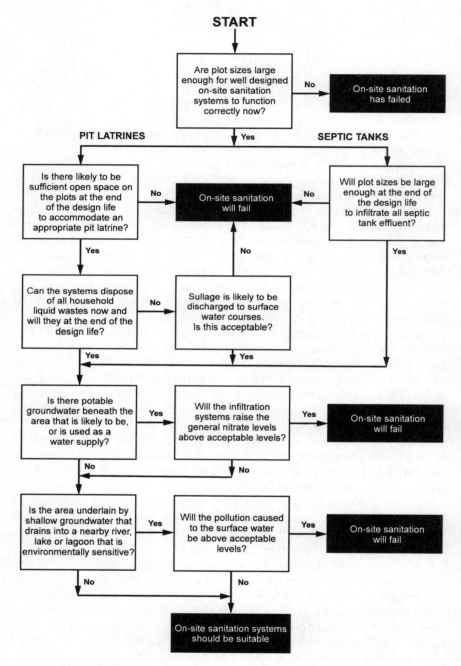

Figure 1.1 *Predicting the likelihood of on-site sanitation failure*

1.1 Reasons for failure of on-site sanitation

On-site sanitation can be considered to have failed for a number of reasons. The main causes are discussed separately below but, as will be seen, they are interrelated and closely connected to rises in water consumption. Figure 1.1 shows a simple chart for deciding whether on-site sanitation systems are likely to fail. In practice the chart would need to be amended to take account of local conditions.

Insufficient plot area

Virtually all on-site sanitation systems rely on infiltration of wastes into the ground. Since the infiltration system is usually constructed on the plot but outside the building, it follows that there must be sufficient open land available on the plot to accommodate the infiltration system.

In general, space for pit latrines will only be a problem in areas of very high-density housing, particularly where there is multi-storey occupancy (simple pit latrines require little more than one or two square metres of land). Insufficient space for septic tanks is usually related to the failure of the infiltration system. Land requirements vary greatly depending on water use and soil conditions but areas of $10 - 100m^2$ for single family systems are not

Table 1.1: Infiltration rates for wastewater into different soil types

Soil type	Description	Infiltration rate (litres/m²/day)
Gravel, coarse and medium sand	Moist soil will not stick together	50
Fine and loamy sand	Moist soil sticks together but will not form a ball	33
Sandy loam and loam	Moist soil will form a ball but still feels gritty when rubbed between the fingers	24
Loam, porous silt loam	Moist soil forms a ball which easily deforms and feels smooth when rubbed between the fingers	18
Silty clay loam and clay loam	Moist soil forms a strong ball which smears when rubbed but does not go shiny	8
Clay	Moist soil moulds like plasticine and feels very sticky when wetter	Unsuitable for soakpits

Source: Adapted from Franceys et al. (1992).

3

unusual. Failure is usually a result of increased water consumption leading to effluent volume exceeding the infiltration capacity of the plot's open land area. Failure may also be caused by plot sub-division when two or more properties produce effluent in a space where only one did before.

Ground infiltration failure

A soil's capacity to absorb liquids with a high organic content such as human wastes varies according to its composition and texture (Franceys et al. 1992). Poorly absorbent soils will infiltrate lower volumes of effluent than more porous soils per unit of soil area. Most ground conditions will dispose of human wastes safely when water consumption levels are low. As water use rises, infiltration rates increase and many soils, particularly those with a high clay and silt content, will block. Table 1.1 gives recommended infiltration rates for domestic wastes in different soil types.

In areas where pit latrines predominate, the problem of inadequate infiltration capacity is commonly overcome by separating sullage from excreta; the excreta can be disposed of in the pit whilst the sullage is discharged to a surface drainage system. Local circumstances will decide whether this should be considered a failure of the sanitation system.

On plots using septic tanks, failure of the infiltration system can be overcome by extending the infiltration area of the sub-surface drainage system. This can only be achieved if there is sufficient open land area available on the plot. If there is not, then the drainage system will fail and excess effluent will overflow into the surface drainage network. Such overflows are a greater health hazard than sullage because the septic tank effluent overflow contains faecal material. The system can therefore be considered to have failed.

Groundwater pollution

Virtually all on-site sanitation systems will pollute the surrounding soil. This is usually only important if the pollution enters a potable and usable groundwater source in sufficient quantity to make the water dangerous to drink without high-cost treatment. Circumstances where such conditions are likely to occur are fully described in Franceys et al. (1992).

Pollution from latrines takes two forms: bacterial and chemical. Bacterial pollution, whilst a direct health hazard, is usually quickly rendered harmless by natural processes. Indeed, provided the bottom of the infiltration system is more than 2m above the water-table, bacterial pollution of groundwater is highly unlikely. Chemical pollution is predominantly nitrogenous and can increase the level of nitrates in the water. Chemical pollution is more problematic than bacterial pollution because it is longer lasting and more difficult to remove.

The pollution from a single domestic latrine is normally minimal, and only a hazard if there is a groundwater abstraction point within 15m of the latrine

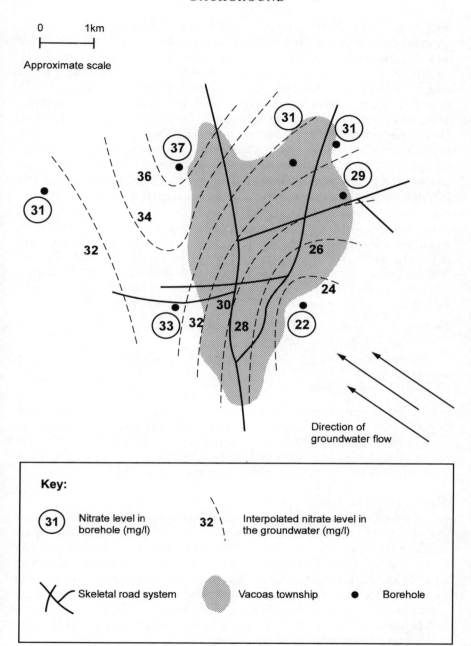

Figure 1.2 *Changes in the nitrate concentration of groundwater as it flows under a community of 56500 people (STI 1993)*

infiltration system (Franceys et al. 1992). A more significant consideration is the cumulative pollution produced by a large number of latrines in a confined area. Shallow groundwater abstracted within the area will almost certainly be contaminated by bacteria and chemicals. Deep groundwater and abstraction points downstream of the area may be contaminated by chemicals. As an example, Figure 1.2 shows the change in the level of nitrate contamination in an aquifer as it flows under a town (Vacoas in Mauritius) with a population of 56500. The aquifer and ground above is a highly-fissured volcanic lava with minimal topsoil. The water-table is approximately 20m below ground and the aquifer has a high velocity. Virtually all properties have septic tanks or pit latrines. It can be seen that the level of nitrates in the groundwater gradually increases as the water flows beneath the township. It then starts to reduce, mainly due to dilution.

The point at which the pollution becomes unacceptable will normally be when the concentration of chemical indicators (such as nitrate) exceed national guidelines within the general body of the aquifer. In countries where national guidelines are absent the World Health Organization recommendations may be used (50mg/l for nitrates). The size of community that produces unacceptable groundwater pollution will be affected by many factors:

O the number and size of infiltration systems;
O the depth to the water-table;
O soil and rock conditions within and above the aquifer;
O aquifer depth;
O groundwater flow rate.

It is worth remembering, however, that when a water source becomes polluted from sanitation systems, it is usually cheaper to relocate the source of the water supply than to remove the sources of pollution. This is because developing new water sources and connecting them to the existing reticulation system is usually much cheaper than sewering a community.

Surface water pollution

Overflowing septic tank drainage systems and sullage from homes using pit latrines will often end up in surface water drainage networks. Even in quite small communities such overflows will quickly destroy the natural flora and fauna, causing unsightly polluted rivers and streams, and possibly becoming a health hazard. Whether or not surface water pollution is a sufficient reason for condemning a latrine system will depend on the local socio-economic conditions and the significance of the water course polluted.

Where a number of similar systems are being compared it may be necessary to find an objective measure of comparison. Tucker and Kimber (1994) suggest measuring the level of pollution (biological oxygen demand or BOD, ammonia and dissolved oxygen) at a fixed distance downstream from the major pollution source, and measuring the distance to a 10 : 1 dilution with

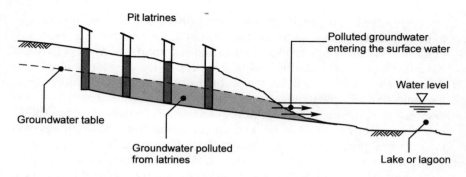

Figure 1.3 *Pit latrines pollute surface waters via the groundwater*

surface water. Such an approach may be satisfactory for small communities, but it is not appropriate for larger ones which have many polluting sources over a large area. It may be more appropriate to compare the total length of each channel within a community carrying a pollution load above a fixed datum.

Surface waters can also be polluted via polluted groundwater. Latrines constructed close to water bodies such as lakes in ground with a high water-table may pollute the surface water if the groundwater flows into it. This has been found to be a problem where communities close to lakes and lagoons have polluted the water via the groundwater (Figure 1.3).

As population densities increase, housing quality improves and the per capita water consumption rises (mainly related to improvements in the water supply). This generates additional sullage water which is frequently discharged into open roadside drains and hence into local water courses and drainage channels. Such practices can lead to unacceptable environmental and health hazards, particularly where nearby communities downstream use the water course for bathing or drinking. The situation is further exacerbated when flush toilets start to be used. In most cases flush toilet wastes can only be disposed of on site using septic tanks and infiltration systems. This requires large plot sizes and porous soils. In low-income housing areas where plot sizes are usually small, the arrival of flush toilets usually signals the end of on-site sanitation as a safe disposal system, and alternatives must be sought.

1.2 Investing in sustainable sewerage

The only satisfactory alternative to on-site sanitation is sewerage: a series of underground pipes collecting and transporting water-borne excreta and sullage from homes to natural water courses. Sometimes sewers also carry commercial and industrial wastes. Sometimes the wastes are treated before disposal. Unfortunately sewerage, as currently practised, is very expensive. Governments rarely have sufficient capital to invest in the large number of sewerage schemes required, and the communities most in need are too poor to be able to repay the capital and running costs. This has led to a number of organizations and communities trying to find new solutions. Most of the trials have taken place in isolation and this has led to the development of very different approaches to solving the problems. All the trials have in common the objective of developing a sustainable and replicable solution to the disposal of liquid wastes from domestic and related properties (such as shops, schools and offices) in low-income communities. They have all selected underground pipes for the removal of wastes from properties, and have re-appraised currently accepted practices and their appropriateness to local conditions. These guidelines aim to promote the idea of sustainable sewerage by drawing together the ideas and experiences gained from these disparate trials in a way that can be used by other practitioners facing similar problems.

The very different approaches adopted in these trials and the environments in which they were tried preclude the development of a single coherent approach to the problem. The ideas are therefore presented here in the form of a 'shopping list'; a series of ideas and suggestions (some of which may appear contradictory) that have been found, under particular circumstances, to improve the sustainability of a scheme. The reader is invited to select ideas which are appropriate to the local circumstances and apply them as necessary. In some countries, some of the ideas may be considered illegal or against current regulations. In such cases the reader is asked to question why that is the case. Is it because they will cause a health hazard? Have they been proven not to work? Or is it just that current laws and regulations were adopted when conditions were very different from those currently being experienced, and are no longer appropriate?

The title, *Sustainable Sewerage*, raises the question: what is meant by sustainable? In this book it is interpreted in two ways. First it is taken to mean 'replicable' in that the scheme can be copied in other surrounding communities. Replication requires that the approach is technically suitable, socially acceptable, and affordable by the recipient communities. If communities cannot repay the cost of the scheme (or a significant proportion of it), then it is probable that municipalities will not have sufficient funds to continue with new schemes. Secondly, it means 'maintainable'. Schemes cannot be operated and maintained over an extended period unless the responsible organization is adequately funded, has sufficient numbers of well-trained and well-motivated staff, and is supplied with appropriate and well-maintained equipment.

This book is multi-disciplinary in nature and, as such, should be of interest to a wide group of practitioners. Much of the book relates to engineering and is therefore primarily aimed at engineers and technicians involved in the design, construction, operation and maintenance of sewerage systems, but it will also be of interest to development and project planners, municipal managers, financial controllers and urban community development workers.

CHAPTER 2
Prioritizing communities' need for sewerage

IN MOST COUNTRIES the demand for sewerage greatly exceeds the resources available to provide it. Factors such as finance, engineering skills and administrative capability all limit the number of new sewerage schemes that can be initiated at one time. There is a need, therefore, to select the schemes which should receive priority and which should be implemented first.

In the past many schemes have been selected on an ad hoc basis with more attention being paid to the political and economic strength of the recipient communities than whether the schemes are likely to be sustainable, cost-effective or needed.

International donors and financial institutions are aware that the failure of many infrastructure projects is because of poor project identification, and this has led to a demand for a more rigorous approach to scheme selection. Such a selection process can be considered in two parts: assembling information which impacts on the selection process; and arranging the information in a way that allows for objective analysis and prioritization. This chapter discusses the major criteria upon which a selection must be based, and suggests a mechanism for objectively analysing those criteria to determine which of a number of schemes should be implemented first.

2.1 Need and viability assessment

The list of factors affecting the prioritization of sewerage schemes is long and will vary from place to place and over time, depending on the conditions prevailing when the analysis is being done. The criteria described below are the most common, but planners should feel free to add or subtract criteria to suit local conditions. As an example, the author undertook a selection analysis in which pollution of coastal lagoons was considered a critical factor. Such a consideration would only be necessary for communities adjacent to lagoons and reefs of national importance. In the majority of situations such a criterion would have little relevance.

As with most design activities, current conditions are only of importance as a guide to what is likely to happen in the future. Sewerage schemes are designed to meet the needs of a community for many years (called the design life) and must be capable of handling the maximum sewage flow, which usually comes at the end of the design life. In general, selection criteria should relate to the conditions expected at the end of the design life rather than those

9

currently experienced. If, however, there are current conditions that are relevant to the prioritization process (such as heavy surface water pollution or schemes proposed for built-up areas which have already reached optimum density) then they should be included.

It is important to remember that all selection criteria must be measurable. The whole purpose of the exercise is to make selection as objective as possible and minimize subjective decision-making. Criteria such as 'consumer demand' should only be used if based on a consumer survey carried out and analysed by a competent organization. The following criteria could form a basis for project selection.

Projected total population

Schemes expected to serve large populations at the end of the design life are generally considered to have a higher priority than those with a lower projected population. This is because large schemes tend to have a lower per capita cost and produce greater social and environmental gains, maximizing the number of people having access to improved sanitation and improving the local environments through reductions in odour and inconvenience from open sullage drains.

Population density

Generally, the higher the population density, the greater the health hazard from poor sanitation and the lower the unit cost of sewerage. Also, as housing density increases and plot sizes decrease, the chances of on-site sanitation systems failing increases.

Failure of on-site sanitation systems

The most common types of on-site system are pit latrines (of varying types) and septic tanks. Readers are advised to consult Franceys et al. (1992) for details of the design and construction of such systems.

The failure of existing on-site sanitation systems is one of the commonest reasons given for needing sewerage. As sewerage is far more expensive than on-site sanitation, the planner should check the causes of any failure (current or projected) before altering the status quo. In many cases failure occurs because of poor design, construction or operation and in such cases, renovation of on-site systems will nearly always be more appropriate than their replacement by sewerage. During a visit to Mauritius the author was asked to comment on a proposal to provide sewerage to a number of communities where on-site sanitation was said to have failed (STI Int. 1993). Site investigation showed that the reason the pit latrines were no longer working was that the pits were full. A programme of pit emptying or replacement was a much cheaper alternative to sewerage. Sewerage should only be considered in communities where on-site sanitation can be proved to have failed irreparably or is likely to fail within the design life (see Chapter 1.1 for details).

Industrial pollution

Although it is rare for a public sewerage scheme to be constructed purely for the treatment of industrial pollution, it is often a significant contributory factor in deciding which community should be sewered. Industrial effluent can be much more concentrated than domestic sewage and it can produce serious pollution of water sources. Some industries produce large volumes of effluent, and its disposal to a communal sewerage network may require sewer pipe diameters to be increased.

If some of the communities being considered for sewerage are industrialized, it will be necessary to find a method for including the impact of those industries in the selection process. A comparison of the organic load (in terms of kilograms of biological oxygen demand per day) produced by industry is one method, but this is more important where sewage treatment is to be included in the scheme. Effluent volume and discharge times may well be more relevant because of their effect on sewer pipe sizes.

Cost

Some measure of the cost of a scheme must be included in the selection procedure. A comparison of total capital costs will identify which schemes are the cheapest and which are within the budget available, but does not show how effectively the money is being spent.

A better measure is the unit capital cost of a scheme. Communities where the wastes are primarily domestic can be measured in terms of the cost of the scheme per person served. Where there is a significant industrial or commercial load the cost per cubic metre of effluent may be more useful.

Operational costs must be considered. Most sewerage networks operate under gravity and therefore the operational costs are approximately proportional to the size of the network. Schemes including pumping will have higher operational costs and this could be taken into account in the selection process.

Most of the factors so far discussed are technical or financial. There will often be other factors relevant to a selection process and peculiar to the particular circumstances. When considering them, it is important that some form of objective measuring and/or estimation criteria are developed.

Tourist impact

In many countries tourism is a major source of employment and foreign exchange. The impact on tourists of unsightly polluted drains, bad odours and 'non-standard' sanitary fixtures can far exceed their potential health hazard. This makes many community leaders consider the provision of sewerage a priority in areas where tourism is or could be an important activity.

Comparison between communities having a tourist interest is difficult; numbers of tourists, length of polluted drains, length of visible polluted drains or pollution of beaches and bathing waters are all possible criteria.

Environmental impact

The impact of a sewerage scheme on the environment may be both positive and negative. Reductions in environmental odour and unsightly pollution within the community may be counterbalanced by increased pollution concentration in the receiving waters with consequent reductions in flora and fauna. Objective evaluation of environmental impact is expensive and requires detailed surveys of the current situation. In this case it is usually sufficient to rely on informed professional judgement.

Affordability

In countries where the demand for sewerage far outstrips the government's ability to provide it, selection based purely on need is not enough. Any long-term policy to provide a service must be based on certain assumptions about how much income the provider will receive from its customers. Where there is equal need, it may only be possible in the first instance to serve communities with a known ability and willingness to pay necessary tariffs, tackling those where higher subsidies may be needed at a later date.

A community's ability to pay for a service can be assessed by comparing the likely tariff with the minimum income levels of the majority of the community. It is normally accepted that a family should pay no more than 2 per cent of its income on sanitation. If a measure of cross-subsidy is assumed within the community, tariffs must be less than 2 per cent of the income of the top 80 per cent of families.

A community's ability to pay for sewerage is not the same as a willingness to pay for the service. Willingness to pay is related more to the perceived importance of the service than to its cost. In communities where sewerage is a high priority, there may be a willingness to contribute a higher percentage of income than the 2 per cent mentioned previously. Conversely, communities having little desire for sewerage will be unwilling to pay 2 per cent of their income for a service for which they have little demand. Estimates of how much a community is willing to pay for sewerage can be obtained from an analysis of household surveys but this can only be a snapshot of current opinion. A community's opinion of what is a reasonable tariff will change over time, depending on changes in general economic conditions, the length of time a service has been in operation, and the services offered to surrounding communities.

It is probably safer to make decisions on cost-recovery based on ability to pay, and include willingness to pay in the ranking process.

Economy of scale

If a number of the communities are close to each other or close to an existing scheme there may be some economy of scale if a single treatment plant can be constructed to serve them all.

Institutional capacity

Sewerage schemes are predominantly implemented, operated and maintained by institutions. Often an institution exists before a scheme commences and it is expected to expand to encompass the new duties necessary for a scheme's construction and operation. An institution's ability to cope with the demands of a new sewerage scheme will greatly affect that scheme's long-term success, both technically and financially. Communities having institutions with the capacity to encompass new commitments and responsibilities efficiently and competently should be favoured in any selection process over communities having institutions that cannot. Decisions on an institution's capacity to cope with added commitments should be based on an institutional evaluation.

Health benefits

One of the main reasons for considering sewerage is to improve standards of health, although not all schemes will produce the same health benefits. Improvements in health will depend on the existing levels of health which, in turn, will partially depend on current levels of sanitation and hygiene practice. It is rarely possible to quantify improvements in health resulting from the provision of sewerage because of the number of variables involved. In most situations it may be assumed that similar schemes will produce similar health benefits.

2.2 Numerical analysis of need and viability criteria

Having decided which criteria affect the ranking of a group of proposed sewerage schemes, it is necessary to determine which of the schemes should have priority for implementation. This book recommends a numerical analysis as follows:

○ Each community is awarded a 'score' for each of the criteria included in the ranking process. For each criterion, a high score indicates that the provision of sewerage to that community is important whilst a low score indicates that it is less critical.
○ Not all the criteria included are of equal importance. It is necessary to weight the scores so that important criteria have a larger impact on the final result than minor ones.
○ A weighted score is produced by multiplying the score by the weight.
○ The total score for a community is the sum of the weighted scores given for each criterion.
○ Communities having the highest scores are most favoured for the immediate implementation of a sewerage scheme.

The magnitude of the scores is unimportant: only the ranking of the communities matters. An example of the selection process is shown in Table

Table 2.1: Prioritizing the provision of sewerage

Town	Projected population			On-site failure			Polluting industries			Unit cost of construction			Tourist impact			Consumer ability to pay			Annual unit O&M cost			Total score
	Sc	Wt	T	Sc	Wt	T	Sc	Wt	T	Sc	Wt	T	Sc	Wt	T	Sc	Wt	T	Sc	Wt	T	
A	10	1	10	1	3	3	1	1	1	4	2	8	1	3	3	4	2	8	5	1	5	38 (8)
B	9	1	9	7	3	21	10	1	10	7	2	14	4	3	12	7	2	14	10	1	10	90 (1)
C	6	1	6	1	3	3	10	1	10	5	2	10	4	3	12	7	2	14	10	1	10	65 (5)
D	3	1	3	1	3	3	1	1	1	2	2	4	10	3	30	10	2	20	5	1	5	66 (4)
E	2	1	2	1	3	3	1	1	1	3	2	6	2	3	6	4	2	8	10	1	10	36 (10)
F	2	1	2	1	3	3	10	1	10	5	2	10	3	3	9	7	2	14	10	1	10	58 (6)
G	2	1	2	1	3	3	5	1	5	2	2	4	4	3	12	4	2	8	5	1	5	39 (7)
H	2	1	2	1	3	3	5	1	5	1	2	2	4	3	12	4	2	8	5	1	5	37 (9)
J	1	1	1	4	3	12	10	1	10	10	2	20	5	3	15	10	2	20	1	1	1	79 (2)
K	1	1	1	1	3	3	1	1	1	2	2	4	1	3	3	1	2	2	10	1	10	24 (11)
L	1	1	1	7	3	21	10	1	10	6	2	12	3	3	9	7	2	14	10	1	10	77 (3)

Key: Sc = Score The impact of a criterion on a town   Wt = Weight The importance of a criterion in the selection process   T = Total The product of the score and the weight

Table 2.2: Projected population

Population range	Score	Population range	Score
15000 - 16299	1	21500 - 22799	6
16300 - 17599	2	22800 - 24099	7
17600 - 18899	3	24100 - 25399	8
18900 - 20199	4	25400 - 26699	9
20200 - 21499	5	26700 - 27999	10

2.1. The table concentrates on technical and financial criteria. It is assumed that other considerations such as health and the environment, which could be included, will be dealt with separately. It is also assumed that the schemes are all designed and constructed using the same criteria.

Scoring for individual criteria

The range of the scoring system for individual criteria and whether the scale from high priority to low priority is ascending or descending is immaterial provided a consistent system is used for all criteria. In the example shown in Table 2.1, a scale of one to ten has been used, with one being minimum importance and ten being maximum. Other ranges are equally valid but they should reflect the level of accuracy with which criteria can be measured, bearing in mind that all the criteria must be measured using the same scale. As an example, the method used for determining the scores for each of the criteria used in Table 2.1 now follows.

The highest and lowest numbers in the range shown in Table 2.2 correspond approximately to the largest and smallest community populations in towns 'A' to 'L' in Table 2.1. Table 2.3 shows individual community scores for projected population at the end of the design life.

The ways that the other scoring ranges were determined is shown in tables 2.4 to 2.9.

Table 2.3: Projected populations for the towns used in Table 2.1

Town	Projected population	Score	Town	Projected population	Score
A	27500	10	G	17000	2
B	26500	9	H	16500	2
C	22000	6	J	16000	1
D	18500	3	K	16000	1
E	17000	2	L	15500	1
F	17000	2			

Table 2.4: On-site sanitation failure

Description	Score
On-site sanitation has already failed	10
On-site sanitation very likely to fail during the design life	7
On-site sanitation may fail during the design life	4
On-site sanitation is unlikely to fail	1

Table 2.5: Polluting industries

Description	Score
More than 50 per cent of the effluent is generated by industry	10
25–50 per cent of effluent is from industry	5
Less than 25 per cent of waste effluent is from industrial sources	1

Note: Since these guidelines relate only to sewerage the effect of industrial effluent strength on treatment costs has been ignored.

Table 2.6: Unit cost of construction

Unit cost (Rs/head)	Score	Unit cost (Rs/head)	Score
40000 - 44999	10	65000 - 69999	5
45000 - 49999	9	70000 - 74999	4
50000 - 54999	8	75000 - 79999	3
55000 - 59999	7	80000 - 84999	2
60000 - 64999	6	85000 - 89999	1

Table 2.7: Tourist impact

Description	Score
Over 80 per cent of the community's income is generated by tourism	10
40 – 80 per cent of income is from tourism	5
No significant tourism income	1

Table 2.8: Consumers' ability/willingness to pay for sewerage

Description	Score
Community can/will repay the full capital and operating costs of the scheme	10
A 50 per cent subsidy is required on the construction cost	7
The community can only afford/is willing to pay operating costs	4
A subsidy is required to make operating costs affordable	1

Table 2.9: Unit annual operation and maintenance costs

Description	Score
No pumping is required	10
Part of the sewerage network requires pumping	5
All of the sewerage has to be pumped to the outfall or treatment plant	1

Weighting

Although all the criteria included should be relevant to the selection process some will be more important than others. Applying a weighting system is a way of reflecting the relevant importance of the criteria in the selection process.

The problem with weighting systems is that it is difficult to apply them objectively. In Table 2.1 for example 'Tourist Impact' is shown as three times more important than 'Projected Population'. This is a reflection of the importance of tourism to the national government in which the example given was carried out. However, to say that it is three times more important is purely arbitrary.

Criteria weights can only be decided upon after discussions with all groups concerned. Since they are so arbitrary it is important that a sensitivity analysis is conducted on the results. This is discussed in more detail in the next section.

Scoring and sensitivity analysis

The total score for a community is the sum of all the weighted scores (as shown in Table 2.1). Communities can be ranked with the highest score being first and the lowest score being last. The high-ranking communities are those most favoured for sewerage. The results of ranking can never be completely objective because of the weighting procedure but confidence in the results can

Table 2.10: Community ranking using sensitivity analysis

Rank	Original ranking	Weighted score	New ranking 1	Weighted score	New ranking 2	Weighted score	Priority
1	B	90	B	93	B	54	
2	J	79	J	84	L	44	High
3	L	77	L	80	C	43	
4	D	66	C	66	J	41	
5	C	65	F	60	F	38	
6	F	58	D	58	D	32	Medium
7	G	39	A	41	A	26	
8	A	38	E&G	37	E&G	23	
9	H	37					Low
10	E	36	H	34	H	22	
11	K	24	K	29	K	17	

be increased by carrying out a sensitivity analysis. This is done by looking at the effects on ranking caused by changes in the weighting. Select the criteria most open to subjective interpretation. Change the weights of those criteria slightly, recalculate the final scores and re-rank the communities. Comparisons between the ranking order for different scoring and weighting scenarios will indicate the level of confidence that can be given to the results. Minimal changes in ranking order indicate a high degree of confidence in the results. Conversely, wide variations in ranking will indicate that the results should be treated with care. Table 2.10 shows the effect of reducing the weighting for tourist impact from three to two and increasing the weight for unit cost of construction from two to three (New Ranking 1) and setting all the weights to unity (New Ranking 2).

Table 2.10 shows that, with the exception of town 'J', the change in weighting numbers has very little effect on the overall ranking of the communities; therefore the results can be accepted with confidence. The actual numbers are of little relevance, only their relative size.

To summarize: a matrix is an excellent method of deciding the order in which communities should be provided with sewerage. By selecting communities using criteria based on need, benefit and cost, the steps in the process can be justified and the final results can be described mathematically. The method is not absolute. It will not select the single most needy community for sewerage. It will, however, segregate a group of communities into those which can cost-effectively obtain the greatest benefit from sewerage and those with less need or requiring greater subsidy. There will normally be a group in the middle (as has occurred in the example) for which the costs and benefits from sewerage make its provision optional. The individual ranking within that group is irrelevant. The selection process described here is primarily technical and financial. Environmental and health considerations also have a place in the selection process. These could be included in the matrix or considered separately. Reference is made to World Bank Technical Paper 140 (1991) for further details of these areas.

CHAPTER 3
Designing conventional sewer networks

THIS CHAPTER IS provided for the benefit of planners and managers who may not be aware of the conventional approach to sewerage design and hence will not be able to appreciate how much the ideas detailed in the rest of the book vary from accepted practice. The section concentrates on design in the upper reaches of sewerage networks, i.e. around buildings and near to sewer ends since this is the area containing most of the sewers and where the rest of this book concentrates. Figure 3.1 shows a typical sewer section in the upper reaches of a network. The terms used for the individual components are not universal but they are those that are used in the rest of this book. Definitions can be found in the Glossary of terms, Appendix 1.

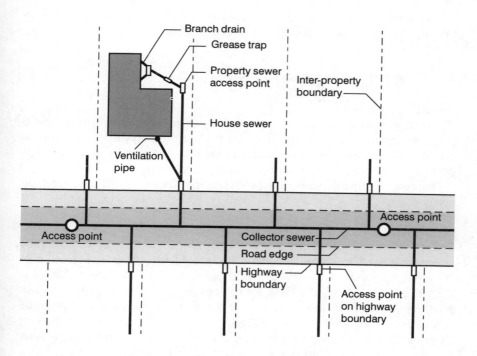

Figure 3.1 *Typical layout of the upper reaches of a sewer network*

Examples from UK practice are used in this chapter to illustrate a typical 'conventional' approach to sewerage design. Other developed countries use methods which are substantially similar.

Sewer design in the upper reaches of a system is usually divided into two parts: building drainage and sewer design.

Building drainage is concerned with pipes laid within and around a property. Pipe sizes and routes are designed to cope with wastewater flows which increase dramatically when an appliance or group of appliances discharges waste. The pipes must therefore be capable of carrying large volumes of waste for short periods. Much of the design is based on past experience and assumes that properties have the numbers of fittings and waste production rates expected in industrial societies.

Sewer design is concerned with pipes constructed for communal use within the highway boundary. It is based on a combination of empirical regulations governing such things as minimum pipe size and gradient and uses hydraulic design based on assumptions of average variations in sewage flow rate.

Whilst building drainage design and sewer design have proved successful, they are often inefficient and costly and may not be appropriate in developing countries. Where water use is low, much of the flow in sewer networks falls in the region between the two approaches, after the effluent leaves the property but before the flow is large enough to provide a continuum. It is in this region that much of this book will concentrate.

3.1 Types of sewerage systems

Separate systems

These are designed to carry foul flows only, from toilet, kitchen and bathroom areas. Storm runoff is excluded. In practice, it is extremely difficult to exclude all storm flows, particularly when sewers are installed after houses have been built unless alternative provision is made to deal with storm flow.

This book is primarily concerned with sewage effluent flowing in a separate system.

Combined systems

These systems are designed to carry both foul and storm flows and thus remove the need for separate storm drainage systems. Except where rainfall is very light, storm flows will tend to be very much greater than foul flows. This leads to two problems. First, for most of the time, sewers will carry only relatively small foul flows and there may be problems with deposition of solids. Secondly, there will be a need to cope with large storm flows at treatment plants and pumping stations. For these reasons combined systems are rarely constructed nowadays. Nevertheless they may be an option in upgrading areas where limited space precludes the provision of separate foul and storm systems. In such cases, provision must be made for separating foul and storm flows before treatment.

3.2 The movement of solids in pipes

Flow regimes

Effluent flow in the upper reaches of a system is marked by extended periods of minimal or no flow interspersed by short periods of high discharge. Lower down the network the increasing number of contributory points produces a virtually continuous flow of effluent which varies throughout the day. It tends to be a minimum in the middle of the night and a maximum at some time during the day. The exact time at which the maximum and minimum flows occur depends on local patterns of domestic water use, the quantity and type of industrial effluent and the distance of the sewer from the source of the effluent. There are two different flow regimes which use different mechanisms for solids transport.

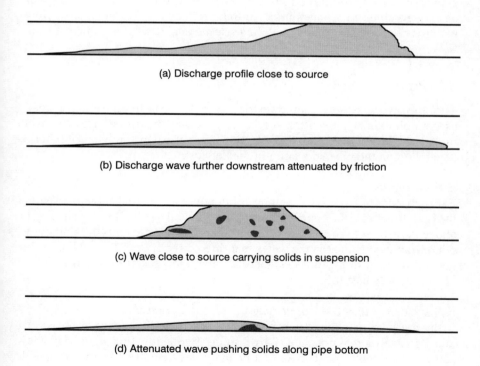

(a) Discharge profile close to source

(b) Discharge wave further downstream attenuated by friction

(c) Wave close to source carrying solids in suspension

(d) Attenuated wave pushing solids along pipe bottom

Figure 3.2 *Solids transport mechanisms in the upper reaches of a sewer network*

Solids transport in the upper reaches

When effluent is discharged into a drain it produces a short, highly turbulent wave which may fill most of the pipe section (Figure 3.2 (a)). As the wave travels along the sewer, friction between the effluent and the pipe wall causes the top of the wave to travel faster than the bottom. This has the effect of extending and flattening the wave (Figure 3.2 (b)). This effect is called 'flow attenuation'.

When solids are being carried in the effluent, they are kept in suspension initially by the turbulence in the short wave (Figure 3.2 (c)). As the wave attenuates, the solids settle to the bottom and are pushed along by the difference in water pressure that develops across the solids (Figure 3.2 (d)). Eventually effluent upstream of the solids leaks away and the solids are left behind. The solids will be moved further down the sewer by successive effluent waves until they reach an area where the flow is continuous.

Solids transport lower down the system

Lower down the system the flow is virtually continuous. Most solids will be kept in suspension and carried along by the flow. Any heavier solids will either be pushed along in a way similar to that produced by the attenuated flow mentioned above or else they will be re-suspended during the times of peak flow.

3.3 Pipe size

The objective when selecting sewer pipe sizes should be to keep them as small as possible whilst preventing surcharging (sewer overflows) and frequent blockages. In practice, pipe-size selection is governed by three sets of criteria depending on the pipe's location in the network.

Branch drains

Except for drains from WCs, branch drains are designed so that they can carry the peak flow from the contributing appliances whilst still allowing an air gap above the effluent. The air gap is important because it prevents the siphoning out of liquid contained in the water seal fitted directly after the appliance. In general, branch drains are designed to carry the peak flow when running approximately half full.

House sewers and the upper reaches of public networks

In this area, the major constraint on sewer size is its ability to carry gross solids and its ease of maintenance. Large solids frequently find their way into sewers, either by accident or deliberately, particularly via the WC and property access points. The minimum pipe size is based on experience and is generally set at 75 or 100mm for house sewers and 100 to 150mm for the upper reaches of public networks.

Public sewers in the lower reaches of the network

Lower down the sewer network, the pipe size will be governed by hydraulic capacity. Pipes are selected that will run nearly full when they are carrying the peak flow.

3.4 Pipe gradient

Once the pipe size has been chosen, the pipe gradient is selected to ensure a minimum velocity, known as the 'self-cleansing velocity'. The self-cleansing velocity is that which is considered necessary to keep solids in suspension as the effluent travels through the pipe. It is generally around 0.75m/s. In practice, the pipe size and gradient are manipulated together to obtain the best design.

In the upper reaches, where solids are transported by being pushed along the pipe invert, the pipe gradient is usually based on 'accepted practice'. In the UK, gradients of 1 : 40 to 1 : 80 are quoted for house drains (BS 8301, 1985) and 1 : 150 for collector sewers (WAA 1989), although there is no evidence to show that such steep slopes are necessary.

Until recently, it was thought that the maximum slope of sewers should be limited, to avoid the stranding of solids and scouring of the pipe. Views have now changed, and up-to-date practice is to allow drains to follow the fall of the land where possible, keeping excavation to a minimum. However, high velocities can introduce problems not normally encountered in sewerage design. The main ones are as follows.

○ High flow velocities are usually very turbulent and this causes air to become mixed with the sewage, increasing the volume of flow (called 'bulking').

○ The surface of the sewer can be damaged by corrosion as a result of the release of hydrogen sulphide gas from septic sewage (sewage from which all the dissolved oxygen has been removed – a common occurrence in hot climates). This occurs where the flow is highly turbulent, e.g. where the sewer slope flattens out causing the sewage depth to increase rapidly.

○ Sewage flowing at high velocities contains significant amounts of energy which must be carefully dissipated at the sewer exit. Otherwise there will be sewage backing up in the sewer and steep sewer discharges causing splashing of sewage.

○ Even shallow depths of fast flowing sewage can be hazardous to operatives entering it. Special attention must therefore be paid to safety.

As a general guide, special care will be needed if the velocity when the sewer is half full (in m/s) is greater than or equal to twice the square root of the pipe diameter (in metres). For example, care should be exercised if the velocity in a 300mm diameter pipe flowing half full is equal to or greater than $2\sqrt{0.3} = 1.95$m/s.

Table 3.1: Discharge units for domestic appliances

Appliance	Capacity (l)	Discharge rate (l/s)	Discharge duration (s)	Recurrence use interval T(s)*	Probability of discharge P	Discharge units
WC (9l high level cistern)	9	2.3	5	1200 600 300	0.004 0.008 0.017	7 14 28
Wash basin (32mm branch discharge pipe)	6	0.6	10	1200 600 300	0.008 0.017 0.033	1 3 6
Sink (40mm branch discharge pipe)	23	0.9	25	1200 600 300	0.021 0.042 0.083	6 14 27
Bath (40mm branch discharge pipe)	80	1.1	75	4500 (domestic) 1800	0.017 0.042	7 18
Automatic washing machine	180	0.7	300	15000	0.020	4

*A use interval or recurrent interval (frequency of use) of 1200s corresponds to domestic use; 600s to commercial use; 300s to congested use such as public toilets, schools and factories.

Source: Adapted from BS 8301 (1985)

3.5 Change point for sewer design

Ignoring the design of house drains (since they are not part of the scope of this book), sewer design divides into two sections: the upper reaches where sewers rarely flow at or near capacity and solids are moved along the pipe invert by water pressure; and the lower reaches where pipes frequently run at or near their design capacity and solids are transported in suspension. The point at which the change takes place obviously depends on local circumstances but its location is important as it has considerable impact on pipe sizes and gradients and hence cost.

In most developed countries, the change is deemed to take place at the boundary of the property, since there are usually different design standards for property drainage than for communal sewerage. Sewerage design in the UK is described below, to highlight the changes which occur at this boundary and the confusion which can be caused.

Property drainage
In many countries including the UK, USA and Australia, house sewers are sized using a system of 'discharge units'. This is a method for predicting the discharge from a number of sanitary appliances so that the effect of a

Table 3.2: Relationship between discharge units and design flow rate

Discharge units	Flow (l/s)	Discharge units	Flow (l/s)
10	2.4	50	3.4
14 (Standard property discharge)	2.6	100	3.9
20	2.8	200	4.6
30	3.0	400	5.8
40	3.3	500	6.2

Source: Adapted from BS 8301 (1985)

combination of fittings can be made on effluent flow rates and hence necessary pipe sizes. It is a function of the appliance flow rate, discharge time, period between reuse and the likelihood of coincident discharges. These factors are combined using the theory of probability and they produce results similar to those shown in Table 3.1.

The discharge units for each appliance discharging to a sewer can be added together and the result converted into a flow using Table 3.2. Discharge units vary from country to country since they are dependent on variations in appliances and their perceived regularity of use, so they should not be transferred directly to another country. Discharge units are calculated for the worst case, which is the flow regime immediately after the appliance. There is no allowance for flow attenuation and this tends to produce over-design of pipes, particularly on long sections.

In the UK a maximum of 14 discharge units is considered acceptable for a domestic property (BS 8301 1985). This is equivalent to the flow from one WC, one wash basin and one sink. Since nearly all houses in the UK have more waste-producing appliances than this, it is not clear why a maximum of 14 discharge units has been selected.

Communal sewer design

Communal sewer design is based on determining the maximum flow that a length of sewer is likely to have to carry, and selecting a pipe and gradient that will carry it without surcharging. In the UK, collection of local water-demand data is recommended for design, but in its absence an average of 220 litres per person per day may be used, with a peak factor of 6. The peak factor is the ratio between the average sewage flow rate on a dry day and the maximum expected flow rate at any time during the year.

In new development areas a design peak flow of 4000 litres per dwelling per day is recommended (BS 8005 1987) which is equivalent to 0.046 litres per second. A pipe is considered to be working at design capacity when it is running 75 per cent full (the other 25 per cent is to allow for sewer ventilation and a factor of safety). It is recognized, however, that sewers will not run full at the head of the system, so an arbitrary size and gradient is specified. The minimum pipe size allowed is 150mm at a minimum gradient of 1 : 150 (WAA 1989).

Determining when a pipe is 'running full'

It is possible to demonstrate the discrepancy between results obtained using property drainage calculations and those obtained using sewer design data. The example below looks at a typical sewage pipe and the number of properties which can be connected to it. Using the discharge unit criteria for property drainage, the maximum discharge in a pipe flowing under atmospheric conditions occurs when the ratio of liquid depth to pipe diameter is between 0.75 and 0.8. At greater flow depths, the resistance caused by the top of the pipe exceeds the effect of increased cross-sectional area on discharge.

A 150mm pipe laid at a gradient of 1 : 150 carries approximately 13.6 litres/second when flowing 75 per cent full. This is equivalent to 2000 discharge units (BS 8301 1985). Therefore, assuming 14 discharge units per house, a total of 143 properties can be connected before the pipe will run 75 per cent full at peak flow. Bearing in mind that the calculation of discharge units makes little allowance for flow attenuation, this is probably an under-estimate of the number of properties that could be connected.

If we now consider the problem using the recommended value for peak discharge from a property, we get a different answer. Assuming a peak flow of 0.046 litres per dwelling per second, the maximum number of properties that can be connected is 296. Admittedly, BS 8005 (1987) recommends the use of discharge units for small groups of buildings but the discrepancy between the two methods is large and both approaches are based on assumptions which are not strictly valid in the region of the sewer network being considered.

3.6 Sewer layout

The cost of sewerage depends to a great extent on the length and depth of the sewers. In general, layout should aim to minimize sewer lengths, providing that this does not result in increased depths of excavation or exclude parts of the area from being connected. In practice, sewers are normally constructed within the highway boundary and follow as closely as possible the topography and natural drainage routes.

In order that traffic loads do not interfere with the sewer pipes, there should be an adequate thickness of soil between the top of the pipe and ground level. In the UK that depth is normally 1.2m (WAA 1989).

3.7 Design procedure

The general procedure for designing a sewerage network is as follows.

i) Design the house sewers, ensuring that the pipe is as close to the surface as is allowable at the highway boundary.

ii) Using a detailed map of the area that shows roads and elevations, prepare a sewer layout showing the direction of travel of each sewer length.

iii) Mark the position of all access points and the number of properties or peak flow likely to be received by each sewer length.

iv) Using the minimum design parameters set by the commissioning authority, determine the lengths of sewers that can be constructed using the minimum appropriate pipe size and minimum gradient. If the ground slopes at greater than the minimum slope the pipes will be able to carry a greater flow. The starting depth will be the lesser of the minimum depth of cover or the depth necessary to allow connection of adjacent properties.

v) Design the rest of the sewer network, attempting to keep the sewer as small and as near to the surface as possible, whilst retaining the minimum cover.

vi) Check that the existing trunk sewer network will carry the additional flow. If not, it will be necessary either to amend the development area so as to reduce flow, or to replace some of the existing pipework to carry the new flow.

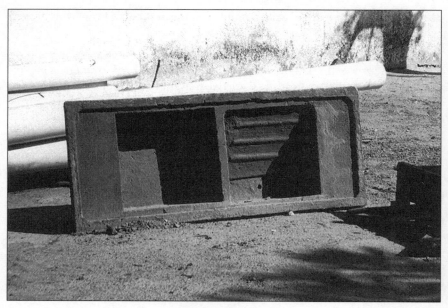

Photograph 1:
Locally made concrete laundry basin, Brazil

Photograph 2:
Locally made concrete toilet pedestals, Brazil

CHAPTER 4
Minimizing capital costs

ONE OF THE most important ways of making sewerage more sustainable is to reduce the cost of its construction. If schemes are cheaper to build, then implementing organizations can construct more for the same money and recipient communities will have less to pay. There are three principal ways in which the cost of sewerage can be reduced: minimizing the number and size of sewerage components; optimizing sewerage design; and improving construction management.

The first section in this chapter looks at savings made by the judicial use of appropriate fittings and materials.

The section on sewerage design investigates ways that the cost of a scheme can be reduced by a reappraisal of the currently accepted norms of design practice in the light of local conditions. The areas of primary concern are the design of sewers in the upper reaches of the network and sewer layout.

The final section examines savings that are possible during the construction process. Emphasis is given to the management and supervision of construction rather than the construction method, since these are the areas where new approaches have had the most effect.

4.1 Sewerage components

Sanitary fixtures
The on-plot component of a sewerage scheme, including the necessary sanitary fittings, can account for up to half of the total cost of construction. Unfortunately, the cost of this component is often ignored during the preliminary investigation, and this frequently leads to a poor connection rate (see Chapter 7) which in turn leads to operational problems and poor tariff returns.

Many countries have set standards for sanitary fittings, but these standards are often inappropriate for current conditions and stifle local manufacture. Basic fittings such as access point covers, squatting pans and laundry basins can easily be manufactured locally from concrete, mosaic cement or ferrocement. Whilst such facilities may not be acceptable to richer residents, they could encourage more poor residents to connect to the sewer.

Transport costs can add significantly to the cost of fixtures. For large schemes, consideration should be given to establishing local manufacture. Whilst support may be required at the beginning, such manufacturing facilities can soon be privatized if the fixtures are acceptable to the customers.

An appliance of particular importance is the toilet, particularly the flushing tank. Toilet flushes in excess of 20 litres are not uncommon. Kalbermatten et al. (1982) have shown that this can account for around 40 per cent of total domestic water usage. Flush volumes of as little as 1.5 litres have proved satisfactory in laboratory trial, 3 litres have been used in Botswana and Lesotho without problems and 4 to 5 litres have been widely recommended. Unnecessarily high flush volumes often limit the water available for other uses and add to the amount of wastewater generated, increasing the cost of collection and treatment.

Pipe materials

Locally manufactured pipe can be very cheap. There are numerous examples of pipes made by local artisans being satisfactory for sewerage schemes and much cheaper than similar imported pipes. The two most common materials for locally made pipes are vitrified (fired) clay and concrete. Vitrified clay is the more robust product and, if properly laid, is durable and not affected by corrosive liquors or gases. Its manufacture does, however, require considerable heat, making the capital investment required greater than that for concrete pipes.

Locally made concrete pipes are often poorly made, making them weak or brittle. They are also prone to attack by the hydrogen sulphide gas which is given off when sewage loses all its oxygen content. Provided that the pipes are properly manufactured and cured, and the sewage contains dissolved oxygen, their use is recommended, since the manufacturing skills required to make them are low, the capital investment is small and the manufacturing plant can be portable.

The type of sewer pipe joint should also be considered. Cheaper locally made pipes often rely on cement-mortar joints. Whilst a cheap material, cement-mortar is very brittle and will fracture if a pipe moves (which it almost always does). Fracture allows the entry of groundwater, silt and tree roots, all of which will cause maintenance problems later. Pipes using rubber O-rings for jointing are more expensive to manufacture but laying is easier. In addition, their ability to accommodate pipe movement without failing causes fewer maintenance problems in the future.

Grease traps

Grease traps should not be confused with gully traps (see Appendix 1). Grease traps are installed along house sewers, although on domestic properties, they are rarely necessary. Only where the quantities of grease entering the sewer are large (such as from a restaurant), or where there is a large quantity of abrasive material used for cleaning utensils, is there a possibility that grease traps will be necessary. The general requirement of grease traps on all domestic properties should be avoided. Field observations show that grease traps are rarely constructed properly, and most residents have little understanding of their purpose or how to maintain them.

Photograph 3: *Combined bathroom and toilet block draining to interceptor tank below, Nigeria. Note the drop in ground level since the block was built.*

Photograph 4: *Sewer network draining the interceptor tanks as shown on page 40. Soil erosion has exposed the pipes and the system is badly damaged.*

Photograph 5:
Rodding eye at the head of a collector sewer, Brazil.

Photograph 6:
Underground junction box with concrete cover lifted, Brazil.

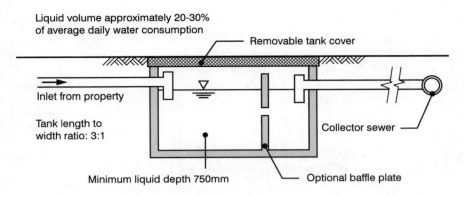

Figure 4.1 *Small interceptor tank with 4-6 hours' retention*

Interceptor tanks

Interceptor tanks are underground storage tanks set in the line of the house sewer, usually near the highway boundary. Effluent from the property enters the tank and the increased cross-sectional area reduces the velocity of flow. This has two effects: some or all of the solids held in suspension settle to the bottom and are not carried over into the downstream sewer network; and the large surface area acts as a damper, evening out the large variations in flow. Interceptor tanks are constructed to reduce maintenance problems in the sewer network and to reduce the total scheme construction cost. They can be divided broadly into two types, small and large.

Small interceptor tanks

Small interceptor tanks have a liquid volume of approximately 250 litres and provide 4 to 6 hours' retention (Figure 4.1). They are installed to trap gross solids before they enter the sewer network and cause blockages, and are used on schemes where per capita water consumption is low and sewer gradients are flat or the quality of sewer construction is poor. They have been used extensively in Orangi, Pakistan, where the idea was conceived. However, they are no longer being installed because the water supply to the area has improved and the completed interceptor tanks were frequently poorly constructed and improperly emptied.

Large interceptor tanks

Large interceptor tanks are more common. They are similar to septic tanks, providing approximately 24 hours' storage (Figure 4.2). Their purpose is to remove all settleable solids from the sewage so that the downstream sewer network can be designed without an allowance for gross solids or siltation. They reduce the peak discharge rate to one approaching the average flow rate and natural processes within the tank provide partial purification of the effluent. Full design details are given in Appendix 2.

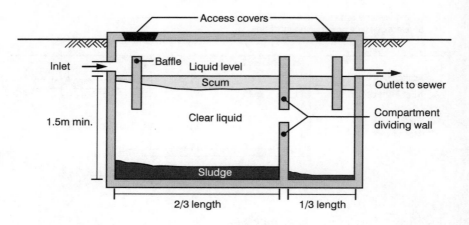

Figure 4.2 *Typical design for a large interceptor tank*

All interceptor tanks require emptying, irrespective of their size, and this must be addressed before commencing with the construction of a scheme. Emptying must be efficient, appropriate and hygienic. This will normally require the provision of mechanical devices such as vacuum tankers. Hand-emptying by bucket is unlikely to be acceptable because of the hazards to the health of the workers and surrounding community during the emptying and carting processes.

Consideration must be given to the final disposal of sludge. If it cannot be treated biochemically, then it must be disposed of in a way that will not pollute the environment (such as sanitary land fill).

Interceptor tanks are normally on private property and the responsibility of emptying them lies with the property owner, but the problems caused by sludge carry-over will be experienced in the downstream communally owned sewer network. This problem is discussed in more detail in Chapter 6.

Access points
It is accepted practice to construct access points at every sewer interception, change in direction or gradient, change in pipe diameter and at maximum fixed distances which are controlled by the equipment used for cleaning. This means that most access points are constructed on house and collector sewers. The concept governing this approach is that access points should be constructed at any point where a blockage could possibly take place, even though most will never be used after completion of construction. Whilst this approach undoubtedly eases maintenance, many of the access points will never be used and it is very expensive. It is common for access points to account for 25 per cent of the capital cost of a scheme (Vines 1991). Economically, it is better to construct schemes without traditional 'manhole' type access points, adding them only as and when required for sewer access.

Some form of chamber is required where sewers meet or change direction so that access can be obtained should it be necessary. The chamber need only be as wide as the sewer diameter, covered by a concrete slab and back filled to ground level (Figure 4.3). Not only does this reduce costs but it reduces the points at which silt and refuse can enter the system.

Some access points will always be necessary, particularly on larger trunk sewers. Consideration should be given to the distance between access points.

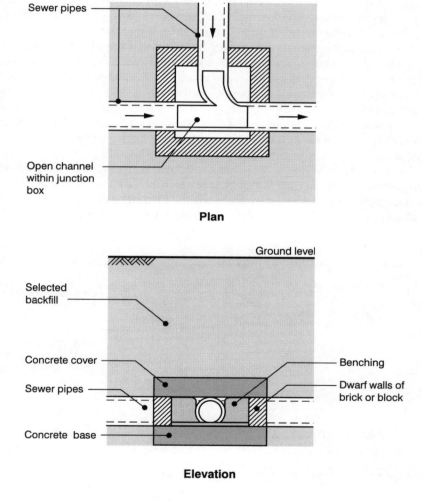

Figure 4.3 *Underground junction box*

Modern sewer-cleaning equipment is capable of reaching up to 300 metres, allowing access-point spacing to be increased. Matching access-point spacing to available cleaning equipment can reduce capital costs, but may increase operating costs where maintenance of highly mechanized equipment depends on expensive imported spare parts.

If 'manhole' type access points must be installed, consideration should be given to reducing their cost. Many standard designs are over-engineered, using excessive amounts of concrete and specifying expensive cast iron covers . Replacing concrete with local stone or bricks and using concrete or stone slabs as covers can produce significant savings. Engineers in Pernambuco, Brazil reduced the cost of access points by 75 per cent by constructing them out of terracotta instead of concrete (Wisemann 1988).

The most common use of access points is for unblocking sewers. This can often be achieved using rodding tubes (Figures 4.4 and 4.5) rather than conventional access chambers. Although rodding tubes do not allow visual access to the sewer, they are generally much cheaper and provide satisfactory sewer access for cleaning purposes, particularly in the shallow house and collector sewers. Each sewer entering or exiting an access point must have its own rodding tube. This makes rodding tubes very appropriate for the heads of sewers and less so for places where a number of sewers combine. Rodding tubes are generally the same diameter as the sewers they serve.

Household access points are generally located either at the boundary of the property or at the junction of the house sewer with the collector sewer. Access points at the property boundary are recommended since they are less prone to vandalism and can be constructed to withstand a lower surface loading.

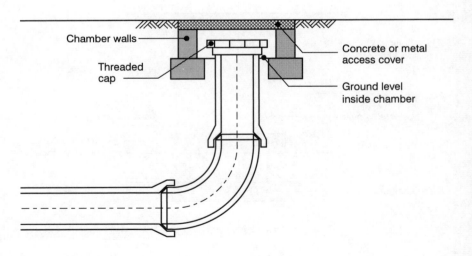

Figure 4.4 *Rodding eye at the head of a sewer*

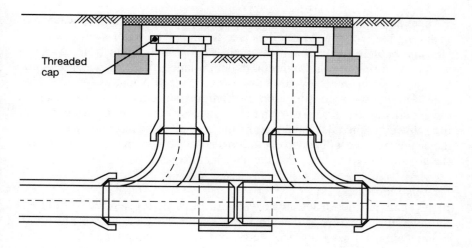

Figure 4.5 *Rodding eyes to replace an access chamber*

4.2 Sewerage design for low-cost systems

By-laws and codes of practice

Much of the work of sanitary engineers is governed by local and national by-laws and codes of practice. Such regulations are there to promote high standards of health within the community and ensure that new structures are capable of carrying out the duties for which they were designed. Unfortunately, many of the codes and laws currently in use in developing countries were imported from other countries with different needs from those of the recipient country.

The areas commonly affected by codes and laws are: water consumption levels; minimum pipe sizes and slopes; the location of collector sewers; and sanitary fittings. Whilst such regulations can often be circumvented for trial schemes, they may have to be reviewed if cost-reducing measures are to be widely used. Any alterations must be realistic and enforceable.

Wastewater flow

If water consumption can be minimized, the size of sewer pipes can be minimized and capital investment can be reduced.

One of the main reasons for considering a sewerage scheme is when increased water consumption leads to problems with sullage and excreta disposal. This usually occurs when the majority of the population have a house connection for water supply and wish to add extra water-using fittings. Many of the water fittings available were designed with little or no consideration for water use.

There are some technical measures that can be taken to reduce water use, including low-volume flush toilets (see Section 4.1), water-saving taps and pressure-reducing valves, but the main savings will come from changing attitudes within the community on the importance of saving water. In some cases this has been achieved by imposing financial penalties for excessive use. Metering water consumption and charging an economic tariff related to the quantity used has been proven to be a successful way of controlling water use. However, the additional cost of meters and the consequential maintenance they require will add to operational costs, so agencies must be sure that the potential savings outweigh the additional costs.

Pipe diameters
In the upper reaches of sewerage systems, solids are transported by differential hydraulic pressure as described in Chapter 3. As Figure 4.6 illustrates, larger diameter pipes require a greater volume of effluent to produce the same depth of upstream flow as a smaller pipe and there is a greater level of leakage around the solids. Because of this, smaller pipes can produce a much higher pressure and are therefore much more efficient at moving solids than larger ones. If pipes are too small, frequent blockages are likely from any large objects deposited in sewers. For networks without interceptor tanks, a minimum pipe size of 75mm is recommended for house sewers and 100mm for collector sewers.

In some cases, larger diameter pipes are cheaper to purchase than smaller ones, but pipes greater than 150mm diameter are not recommended for house connections and the upper reaches of communal sewers because the depth of flow may not be sufficient to transport solids.

Systems designed to receive wastes from interceptor tanks with four to six hours' retention time need only be designed to carry peak flows with no allowance for large objects. Current practice is still to use a minimum size of 75mm but there is no reason why smaller pipe sizes could not be used, provided they can carry the peak hydraulic flow.

Networks installed using interceptor tanks with 24 hours' retention time may be designed to carry average-day flow rates. Currently the minimum pipe size in use is 40mm but there is no reason why smaller diameters could not be used.

It is recommended that sewer pipes between the waste discharge point and interceptor tanks are at least 75mm for toilet wastes and 30mm for sullage.

Sewer slope
In the upper reaches of a sewer network, sewer pipes never run full. The minimum slope is based on experience and is related to the quality of construction (particularly the quality of joints), per capita water use, the volume of silt, the type of wastes carried and the roughness of the pipe. House sewers with diameters of 100mm and gradients of 1 : 1200 have been reported

as working satisfactorily over short distances (Bartlett 1970) but it is unlikely that such flat gradients would be satisfactory if the drains were long or badly laid. Current experience suggests that, unless sewer construction is very poor, minimum pipe slopes of 1 : 167 (0.006) should be satisfactory. Where pipes are smooth, construction quality is good, and water consumption high (greater than 120 litres per person per day), gradients of 1 : 220 (0.00454) could be considered.

Note: In a large sewer, the area of effluent (L^1) surrounding an obstruction is greater than that surrounding an obstruction of the same size in a small sewer (L^2).
Effluent retained by an obstruction will therefore drain away faster in a large sewer than a smaller one. As it is the effluent behind the obstruction that moves it along the pipe, the distance the obstruction moves with each flush will be less in a large sewer.

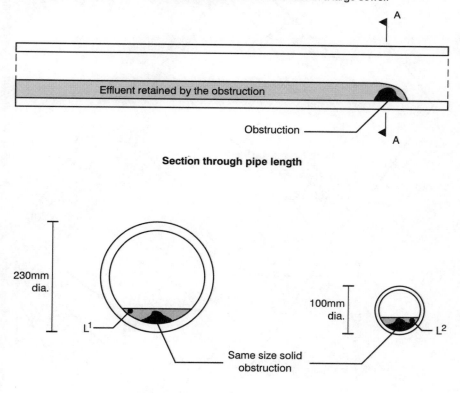

Figure 4.6 *Effect of pipe diameter on solids movement efficiency*

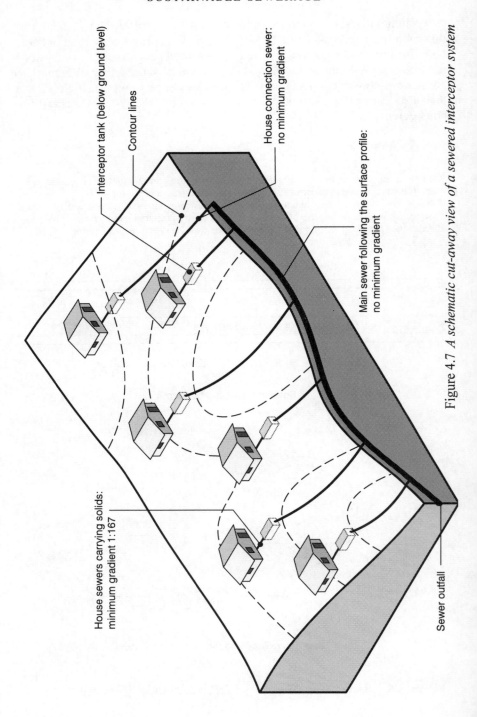

Interceptor tank (below ground level)

Contour lines

House connection sewer:
no minimum gradient

Main sewer following the surface profile:
no minimum gradient

House sewers carrying solids:
minimum gradient 1:167

Sewer outfall

Figure 4.7 A schematic cut-away view of a sewered interceptor system

Further downstream, once sewers have sufficient flow to ensure a self-cleansing velocity at the peak flow at the beginning of their design life, there is no need for a minimum gradient.

Sewer systems served by small interceptor tanks can be laid at a minimum slope of 1 : 220. This assumes that the quality of materials and construction is good and that the interceptor tanks are regularly and effectively desludged.

Pipe systems served by large interceptor tanks do not need a minimum gradient, since the effluent they transport contains no settleable solids. Provided there is an overall positive gradient on the system and all interceptor tanks are above the static water level in the sewer, the pipe can follow the local topography (Figure 4.7). Short lengths of sewer with reflex gradients (sloping away from the outlet) are acceptable, provided they are ventilated and provision is made for emptying. Such systems are completely dependent on the regular emptying of the interceptor tanks for their reliability.

Once a sewer reaches its design capacity, pipe gradients are controlled by the volume of flow, pipe diameter, allowable depth of flow and velocity. Systems without interceptor tanks should normally be designed with a minimum velocity at peak flow of 0.5m/s. Systems with small interceptor tanks may be designed with lower velocities (such as 0.3m/s) but this has not been proven. As mentioned before, systems with large interceptor tanks have no minimum velocity constraint.

The maximum design depth of flow is normally 75 per cent but sewers after interceptor tanks may be designed to run full.

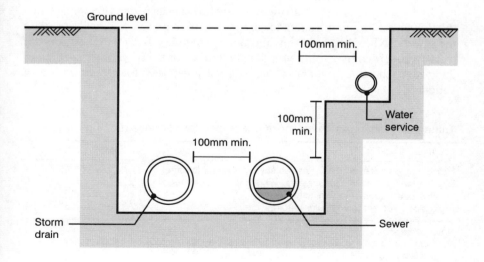

Figure 4.8 *Typical installation of pipework in a shared trench*
Source: AS3500.2 (1990)

Table 4.1: Relative costs of pipes laid at various depths

Depth (m)	Relative cost	Depth (m)	Relative cost
0.5	1.0	2.0	9.75
1.0	3.78	2.5	12.98
1.5	5.69	3.0	16.56

Note: Costs are for excavation per running metre in sandy, silty or clay soils for 150mm pipes.

Source: Adapted from MDU/PNUD (1986)

Minimum pipe depth

The depth at which a sewer is laid has significant cost implications as is shown in Table 4.1. The minimum depth of cover (the distance from the top of the pipe to the surface) is governed by three factors: the pipe's ability to withstand the imposed loads; the relative vertical position of adjacent water mains; and the depth necessary to connect upstream sewers or appliances.

The minimum recommended cover for house and collector sewers is given in Table 4.2.

When water-pipes have to be laid in close proximity to sewers, they should always be above and to the side of the sewer. Figure 4.8 suggests a minimum spacing.

Number of connections before a sewer pipe runs full

There are two mechanisms for the movement of solids in sewers: suspension and hydrostatic pressure. Both methods are fully described in Chapter 3. Once the flow in a sewer is sufficient to carry solids in suspension at peak flow then the sewer can be designed using hydraulic principles. Before that, sewers are usually governed by a minimum diameter and slope. The problem is how to determine when the sewer has achieved a sufficient flow to suspend and carry solids.

Table 4.2: Minimum cover for house and collector sewers

Location	Minimum cover (m)
Flexible pipes such as uPVC not subject to vehicular loading	0.45*
Rigid pipes such as vitrified clay not subject to vehicular loading	0.3
Flexible pipes subject to vehicular loading	Approx. 0.5**
Rigid pipes subject to vehicular loading	Approx. 0.5**

Note:
*   Pipes could be laid with less cover provided they are protected from gardening and landscaping activities.

**   The depth of cover for areas subject to vehicular loading is a function of the strength of the pipe, the type of pipe bedding and the imposed loads. Reference is made to BS 8301 (1985) for more details.

Photograph 7: *Collector sewer network with access chamber at every house connection. The network has become exposed by soil erosion. The alleyway follows a natural drainage path, Pakistan.*

Photograph 8: *Threading a condominial sewer through the rear of a housing block in North-East Brazil. Note the good practice of bedding the sewer on granular material.*

Table 4.3: Minimum number of connections required to produce a velocity of 0.5m/s at peak flow

Housing type	Pipe diameter (mm)	Pipe slope	Min. no. of connections	Proportional depth of flow	Max. no. of connections
High income	100	1:100	11	0.30	53
housing (peak flow	100	1:167	20	0.45	41
assumed to be	150	1:200	11	0.21	110
0.092 l/s/house)					
Medium income	100	1:100	17	0.30	83
housing (peak flow	100	1:167	31	0.45	64
assumed to be	150	1:200	18	0.21	172
0.058 l/s/house)					
Low income	100	1:100	25	0.30	120
housing (peak flow	100	1:167	45	0.45	93
assumed to be	150	1:200	26	0.21	250
0.040 l/s/house)					

Notes:
High income per capita discharge assumed to be 200 l/day.
Middle income per capita discharge assumed to be 120 l/day.
Low income per capita discharge assumed to be 75 l/day.
Peak flows assume a family size of six, a peak factor of six and an infiltration rate of 0.0083 l/s/house.
Pipe discharge assumes a ks value of 1.5mm and a minimum velocity of 0.5m/s.
Maximum numbers of connections assumes the sewer is running 75 per cent full.

The determination of the number of properties that can be connected to a collector sewer before it is likely to transport solids in suspension is a function of pipe diameter and slope, water use, length of house connection and distance between connections. As has already been described in Chapter 3, there are two accepted methods of carrying out the calculation, both based on assessing the property flow at peak time. The first method assumes an average household daily flow and multiplies it by a peaking factor. The second assesses the probability of a number of appliances discharging at one time and the resultant flow rate. The former is most appropriate for sewers receiving wastes from a large number of properties and the latter for flow in individual or small groups of house sewers. Neither calculation is strictly appropriate in the intermediate region, which is the head of collector sewers. Of the two methods, the latter is probably the more accurate, but it requires detailed information on appliance discharge rates and probable frequency of use. It is likely that neither of these values is easily available.

For simplicity of design, the use of a factored average flow rate has been found to be acceptable (that is, multiplying the average by a factor based on published data or experience to give the average at peak times), and Table 4.3 suggests the number of house connections required before sewage flow is great enough to carry solids in suspension. The table is suitable for systems without interceptor tanks or after small interceptor tanks. Calculations should be based on initial peak flow rates, which are lower than design peak flow rates. Sewers should then be checked to ensure their ability to carry the design peak flow.

Sewer systems with large interceptor tanks may be designed from the head of the sewer to carry the average daily flow plus some allowance for seepage of water from the ground. As there are no solids in suspension, calculations of pipe capacity can be based entirely on the summation of average daily flows from each property.

Sewer layout

Normal practice is to lay collector sewers in the public highway (Figure 4.9). This has been preferred by engineers because most of the sewer network is easy to reach for maintenance and there is little need to purchase expensive rights of access to private property. This argument reflects the commonly held belief among practising engineers that a sewer network starts at the collector

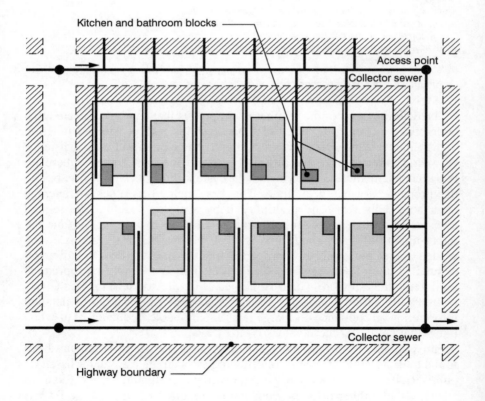

Figure 4.9 *Conventional layout of a collector sewer network*

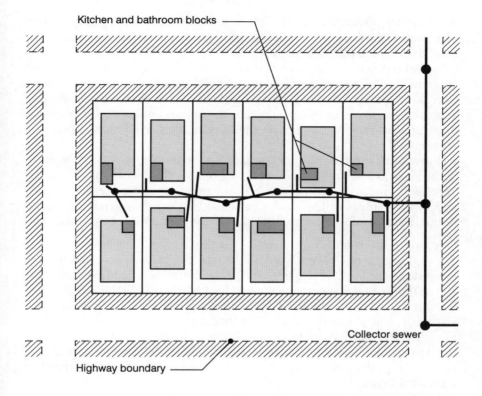

Figure 4.10   *Back-service collector sewer*

sewer. It ignores the additional costs (and lengths of sewer) that may be required by the property-owners to connect their appliances which are commonly at the rear. It also means that the sewer must be deep to prevent damage from vehicles and to allow for the long house connections.

If the collector sewers are laid at the rear of the properties, in alley-ways or across plots (not accessible to vehicles), the sewer can be shallower, since there is little imposed loading (Figure 4.10). In addition, the house connections will be much shorter. Reductions in total pipe length (house sewers plus collector sewers) of as much as 50 per cent have been recorded (UNHCS 1986). Furthermore, responsibility for maintenance of the collector sewer can be transferred to the residents. Reductions in capital and operational costs can be considerable. Costs as low as 9.5 per cent of the cost of an equivalent conventional sewerage network have been recorded and savings exceeding 50 per cent are common (Vines 1991).

Back-service collector sewers are most appropriate where blocks of houses back onto each other and house plots are long and narrow. In such cases the buildings commonly take up the full width of the plot, making construction of a sewer to the front of the property difficult, but providing spare land at the rear which is unlikely to be developed.

Problems associated with such systems are sewer failure due to the construction of buildings over the sewer line and arguments between residents over the responsibility for clearing blockages. Both problems can be prevented by the provision of clear guidelines prior to construction on responsibility and maintenance and by the enforcement of building and planning regulations.

Where back-service collector sewers are not possible, consideration could be given to constructing the sewers in front gardens or the footpath. The benefits from construction in the footpath are minimal. Sewers constructed under front gardens will reduce house connection lengths and possibly sewer depth. They also allow the transferral of maintenance responsibility to residents.

Pumping stations and trunk mains

The closer the sewer system's outfall is to the properties served, the cheaper the system will be. On the other hand, if the outfall is too close (such as the end of the road) the environmental and health benefits will be minimal.

If the cost of sewage treatment is included, the comparison is less clear-cut. Generally, a large number of small treatment plants will be more expensive to construct, require more land, be less efficient and require a larger workforce to operate than a single large plant. Whether the savings in treatment cost outweigh the additional cost of trunk sewers or pumping will depend on individual conditions.

Small drainage systems with localized treatment (often called micro-drainage systems) have the advantage that they are suitable for incremental development (Figure 4.11). As much as possible, micro-drainage systems should be designed in accordance with a regional master plan so that any future investment does not require duplication of existing infrastructure, provided doing so does not create problems with disposal of the effluent.

Sewage treatment

Many sewerage schemes in developing countries do not incorporate sewage treatment. Whilst this cannot be recommended, economic constraints require developing countries to prioritize their investment. In such circumstances, deferring construction of treatment plants provides a significant cost saving and releases funds for sewering other districts in a community. In many communities, demand for sewage treatment has a much lower priority than sewage collection as the majority of the benefits accrued by the recipient (and often paying) community comes from sewage collection rather than from sewage treatment.

Such thinking favours micro-drainage systems with little or no treatment which have the potential for connection to a trunk collection and treatment network at a later date.

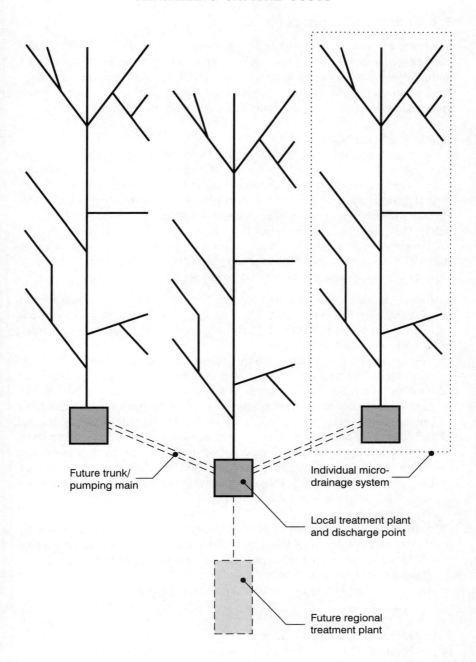

Future trunk/
pumping main

Individual micro-
drainage system

Local treatment plant
and discharge point

Future regional
treatment plant

Figure 4.11 *Micro-drainage systems*

4.3 Construction project initiation

Sewerage projects can be initiated by government agencies such as municipalities, water authorities or regional governments, by external organizations including non-government organizations (NGOs), aid agencies, development groups, or by the recipient community or any combination of these. Each group has advantages and disadvantages as a lead organization.

Government agencies

Government agencies are probably the most common organizations for initiating sewerage even if they do not actually implement its installation. They have the advantage of access to trained and experienced personnel, large capital grants and legal powers for recouping expenditure. They are also the agencies whom most communities expect to implement sewerage. Unfortunately, they are often bureaucratic, slow, inefficient, corrupt and bounded by inappropriate regulations. This leads to the slow implementation of expensive schemes that often cannot be adequately maintained. There are, however, a number of ways that they can reduce construction costs.

○ Municipalities often have under-utilized direct labour organizations and expensive capital equipment. Their standing costs must be met irrespective of whether they are used. Secondment of spare capacity to construction projects can reduce costs.
○ Treatment plants are nearly always constructed on municipal or government land. The land often has to be purchased from the private sector or another government department. In the latter case, it may be possible to negotiate a long-term lease of the land at favourable rates rather than purchase. It may even be possible for the land to be provided free of cost.
○ Schemes implemented by government agencies usually have some level of political support or they would not be implemented. Such support can be used to persuade the agency to reduce costs by changing its methods of project implementation. Changes to local by-laws, contract-letting procedures and approved construction techniques are all areas where cost savings can be made.
○ Affiliation of a project to one political party may speed up implementation if that party is in power. Should the government change, the close party ties could persuade the incoming party to disassociate itself from the project, leading to its demise and the loss of a large capital investment. Cross-party support should be assured before a project commences.

External organizations

External organizations can reduce costs by capitalizing on their independence of government. Communities often consider government departments to be responsible for providing sewerage. When a community is asked by government to invest directly in a scheme it may refuse, considering it a reneging of government responsibility. External agencies are not usually linked with a statutory duty to provide sewerage and therefore when they do get involved they can often persuade communities to co-operate with them.

External organizations are also more able to obtain support from third party groups such as trade unions or private industry. The support may be in the form of a capital grant, subsidized material or technical support. The latter may introduce new ideas and technologies which can impact on implementation costs.

External organizations may be less bureaucratic than government ones, simplifying management and decision-making. They can experiment with ideas that may not be acceptable under current regulations. Their lack of political accountability may allow more objective decision-making and financial stability.

The main problems with using external organizations are related to long-term operation and maintenance and replicability. Many agencies, particularly those funded by international aid, are not interested in long-term operation and maintenance. Once the scheme is completed, they want to hand it over to a local organization, which may cause problems. Experimental schemes, where innovations have been tried that do not comply with current regulations, may not be accepted for maintenance by local municipalities. Maintenance organizations set up within communities may collapse because of apathy from the residents and lack of external support after the external agency leaves.

External agencies are not very good at replication. The lessons learned from a scheme are only of use if they are incorporated in other schemes. External agencies, by their very nature, are not able to take on widespread implementation of sewerage. If the ideas are not taken up by the organizations normally responsible for sewerage then they will be lost and there will be no long-term gain.

For these reasons, external agencies must work in partnership, either with the regular implementing agency or with the recipient communities. Their input should always be seen as short-term which is only viable if the recipient community has institutions which can take on the maintenance of the sewerage installation.

Recipient communities

Community-led projects tend to produce a system that the community desires at a price it can afford. Many communities have poor project-management skills leading to slow implementation rates and frustration on the part of contractors and suppliers. Furthermore, they may offend local politicians and influential contractors who may be able to hinder the programme.

Community-led projects are rare. They only take place in communities where the government has shown that it will not carry out its obligations and there is a genuine desire for sewerage. Such schemes tend to be constructed piecemeal, with little overall planning, and little concern for environmental pollution or for their effect on neighbouring communities. Their main advantages are that they are very cheap (see Table 4.4) and maintenance is virtually guaranteed by the community.

4.4 Construction management

Where possible, co-ordinating sewer construction with other investments such as water supply, drainage or road-making will reduce the cost of construction, preventing the cost of double excavation and road reinstatement and eliminating the disturbance of other utilities.

Contracts and contractors

Projects constructed using large contractors tend to ease construction supervision. Large contractors usually have project management skills and good quality equipment. Their staff tend to be skilled and have more experience of sewerage construction tasks. They are more permanent and therefore easier to contact after the project is complete. However, large contractors tend to have large overheads, inflating the total cost of a project. They often have strong political connections that may enable them to get away with less competitive charges.

Small contractors or local residents usually have lower overheads, making a project cheaper. However, their skill level is usually lower (which may have operation and maintenance implications) and the larger number of separate contractors required means more co-ordination by the implementing agency.

Experience demonstrates that large contractors are better for large projects that have to be constructed in their entirety, such as treatment plants, pumping stations and trunk mains. Small contractors are better for small projects or where the project is to be implemented in small, initially unconnected sections such as collector and house sewers.

Table 4.4: Comparison of construction and supervision costs of collector sewers in Orangi, Pakistan

Construction and supervision	Length of sewer (m)	Cost per metre (Rs)
Built by small contractors, supervised by community group	89536	52.07
Built by small contractors, supervised by individual user groups	189926	49.97
Built by large contractors, supervised by local government agency	34267	295.08

Source: Adapted from OPP (1989)

Construction supervision

Supervision of construction is usually the responsibility of the implementing agency or its designated representative. A number of projects have used community institutions to supervise construction. This approach can reduce supervision costs and the close interest shown by residents in the quality of their own sewer can increase construction quality. Resident supervision appears to work well with small contractors, particularly where residents have contributed to the construction cost. Such an approach does have training implications as residents may not understand what the construction entails or what the final job should look like. They will require training in construction supervision and small project management.

Community mobilization

Involving the community in the construction process can reduce costs, speed up implementation and, as will be seen in Chapter 5, improve operation and maintenance. The ways that a community can be mobilized to become involved are almost as numerous as the schemes in which they have taken part. Vines (1991) discusses in detail the ways that communities have been mobilized and the different contributions they have made to a scheme's implementation.

CHAPTER 5
Maximizing uptake of sewerage facilities

THE HIGH INVESTMENT cost of sewerage is completely wasted if properties are not connected to the system. The most common reasons for residents not connecting to a system are: inadequate funds; low priority; confusion about individual and corporate responsibilities; and conflict between tenant and landlord. This section will concentrate on measures to reduce connection costs, raise a community's willingness to connect, and resolve problems of responsibility for connecting in rented accommodation.

5.1 Reducing connection costs

Engineers are frequently unaware that the on-plot component of a sewer network costs almost the same as the unit cost of construction of the communal sewer network. When considering whether a community can afford to pay for sewerage it is important to include the cost of the on-plot component.

Physical measures
Physical measures such as lower-cost sanitary fittings and relocation of the collector sewer to reduce connection lengths and depths are discussed in detail in previous chapters.

Providing subsidies
Providing a subsidy for the on-plot component of a sewerage scheme is generally considered by implementing agencies to be beyond their responsibility. Even when connection costs are minimized, many poor families will be unable to find sufficient funds to pay the full cost of connecting and the scheme will be under-utilized. It may therefore be in the interest of the implementing institution to assist with the cost of connections.

Subsidies should not be considered until a sanitary survey has been completed. The survey should collect data on: the type and number of sanitary fixtures already installed on the plots; the location and length of any existing pipework; and income levels and property values. A comparison can be made between the likely cost of connecting (on-plot and off-plot costs), income levels and property values. It is generally considered that residents should only be expected to spend about 2 per cent of their household income on sanitation (Kalbermatten et al. 1982). An assessment can be made as to whether a subsidy is necessary.

The options for providing a subsidy are numerous and include:

○ Providing the sewer connection from the property boundary to the collector sewer at no cost.
○ Supplying basic sanitary fittings such as toilets, sewer pipes and access point covers at below market price.
○ Giving long-term interest-free loans.
○ Providing income-related credits or cash to offset the cost of connection.
○ Offering to connect all fittings installed at the start of the project at a reduced rate. This optimizes connections from individual properties early in the life of the scheme.

Measures such as free sewer connections and low-interest loans will benefit all residents, whilst subsidizing basic fittings or providing income-related credits targets the subsidy to the poorer families.

There are a few examples of the implementing agencies paying all of the on-plot costs (e.g. Brotas, Brazil) but this is very expensive and such a scheme is unlikely to be replicable.

5.2 Increasing demand for sewerage

A community's knowledge and understanding of sewerage may be very variable. It is important that at an early stage in the project the community's knowledge-base is evaluated. Any evaluation should include data on the priority placed on sanitation by the community. The most common reasons given for a lack of interest are: a lack of awareness of the benefits of sewerage; ignorance of health risks from existing facilities; worry about the damage and disruption that sewer construction would produce; and cost. It is only after such data has been evaluated that an appropriate awareness-building campaign can be developed.

Community education is not just about explaining the importance of sewerage. It also includes information on potential sources of financial and technical assistance, the division of financial and operational responsibility, expected costs, implementation time-scale and areas of cost uncertainty. All of these factors should be introduced to a community as early in a project as possible to foster a feeling of openness by the project staff. Eventually all this information will have to be defined in some form of agreement but this will be discussed later.

Some of the ways that a community can be made more aware of the importance of sewerage and how it could contribute to a scheme's success are described below.

Meetings

Meetings are one of the best ways of communicating detailed information. Initially a meeting can be large and provide a general introduction to sewerage and its benefits and discuss what different parties will be expected to

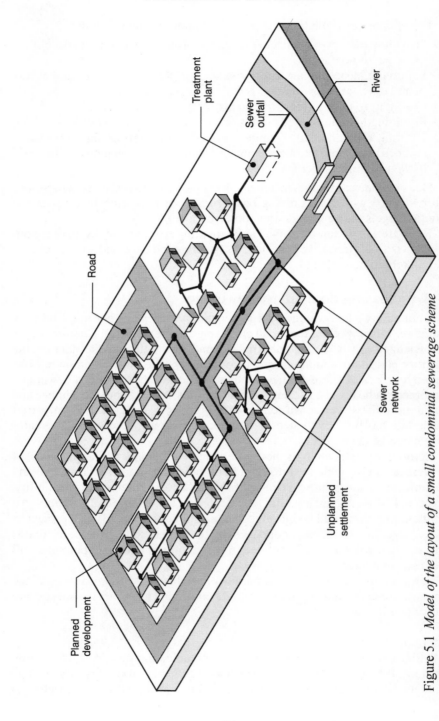

Figure 5.1 *Model of the layout of a small condominial sewerage scheme similar to the one used for demonstrations in Rio Grande do Norte, Brazil*

contribute. It can also introduce the different options for sewerage with descriptions of their relative merits and costs. At a later stage a meeting can be used to discuss general layout, implementation schedules, detailed costs and cost-recovery options.

Most of the detailed work will take place in small meetings. Residents should be divided into groups of about 20 families, often those families living in a block or on either side of a road. These meetings will discuss topics such as detailed layout, location of access points, routing of house connections, maintenance responsibilities and group contributions to the construction cost.

Meetings will also be required with individual families to discuss improvements to the sanitary facilities, layout of house sewers, location of access points, cost implications, payment methods and maintenance requirements.

Models

Many people find sewerage an abstract idea and their understanding can be improved by showing them models. Models may be small, showing details of a particular aspect of a proposal, such as the sewer layout around a house or within a housing block. It could also show the typical layout of a whole scheme (Figure 5.1) and be used to explain the importance of individual components and how they relate to each other.

Existing schemes can act as models. Visits by community leaders or the whole community to an existing scheme can illustrate the effects the scheme has had on individual families, the community and its environment. Many people find that looking at an actual scheme does not give them a full understanding of how the parts fit together to make the whole project. Desktop models are often still necessary to give an overall picture of the proposals.

Large numbers of people visiting a small community to look at its sewerage scheme can be very disruptive. It may be necessary to give a substantial discount to these demonstration communities to persuade them to accept the visitors.

General publicity

Schemes encompassing large parts of a town will benefit from more general awareness-building such as can be provided by presentations on local radio or television, articles in local newspapers, visits by project staff to local schools, visits to women's groups and clinics, community film or slide shows, theatre presentations of sketches including sanitation and health problems, leaflets and posters.

Emphasizing positive impacts

Residents may not be aware of all the benefits that the scheme could bring. Benefits are likely to include:

○ Improved health leading to reduced expenditure on medication.
○ Improved appearance of the plot and surrounding streets.
○ Saving in embarrassment about dirtiness or smell when guests visit.
○ Increased trade for local shops because the shopping environment has improved.
○ Escape from the inconvenience of traditional sullage disposal methods or leach pit emptying.
○ Increased property values.
○ A modern bathroom with flush toilet.
○ Fewer community quarrels about waste water.
○ Fewer mosquitoes allowing better sleep.

Confronting negative issues

A lack of interest in a project may be due to negative feelings in the community. Such feelings must be brought out and discussed openly as ignoring them will only damage the project.

Common problems are: insecurity of tenure; low priority because poor water quality or the lack of electricity supplies may be deemed more important; a feeling that an inferior sewerage system is being offered compared to that offered to high-income areas; and low investment priority (a new television is often considered more important than a toilet). Such issues should be discovered during the initial social survey, but if they are not, they must be confronted as soon as they are recognized.

All construction work causes disturbance to the environment and inconvenience to local residents. Although this cannot be avoided, the amount of likely disruption should be explained, together with the measures that will be taken to minimize it and to reinstate any damage.

Offering user choice

The wider the choice offered to residents in terms of sewerage options and household fittings, the more communities will be attracted to the scheme.

If possible, road or block groups should be given options for the level of service. Options ranging from 'conventional' sewerage, centrally maintained, to a much simpler system maintained by the community can be explained, together with their cost implications. The group can select which option they would like. At household level, residents can be offered a range of basic, possibly subsidized, sanitary fittings and different repayment options.

This type of approach requires a flexible institution capable of managing a large number of small groups with differing funding options and levels of service. Some institutions have succeeded with this approach. In North Brazil, the city of Petrolina offers the community options for the location of the collector sewer in: the road; the footpath; the front garden; the back garden. Each option has differing capital costs and community maintenance requirements.

Linkage with other projects

If sanitation has a low priority in the community, construction of sewers could be linked to another service or utility that has a higher priority. The most common example is that found in many parts of Brazil where municipalities will not tar-seal a road until the houses adjoining it have been sewered. There is no reason why this principle could not be linked to other services such as water-connection to houses, building a school or clinic, providing a bus service, or refuse collection.

Choosing a name for a community project

The name of a product can be just as important in influencing attitudes as the product itself. An excellent example of this is 'Condominial Sewerage'. The name was originally chosen because it fitted the way the system worked, but its introduction in Brazil coincided with a popular television programme about rich people living in a condominium. The connection between the two was made, and it had a tremendous impact on the acceptability of the system.

Campaign implementation

The most successful community-education programmes related to the provision of sewerage have been led by community or social workers rather than engineers.

Even more important than the background of the lead staff is their continuity during the project cycle. Confidence in the future success of a project is often related to confidence and respect for the individuals promoting it. If the promoters are not residents of the area, which they should be if possible, the community will need time to develop a rapport with them. It is a good policy to keep the same promoters throughout the whole project cycle.

5.3 Legal issues

Enforcement of connections

In areas where the community is known to have an income capable of supporting their contribution to a new scheme, legal enforcement of connections could be considered. It is unusual to use such an approach but it could be used to persuade a minority of families who are unwilling to be connected. Enforcement will only work if there is the political will to ensure that the laws are enforced, if the laws have general social support and if the enforcing institutions are strong enough to implement them. A monetary fine or disconnection from the water supply are options which have been applied to residents who do not connect, though consideration should first be given to their reasons and to possible remedies.

Other agencies have encouraged connection by charging a sewer tariff on all families who could connect to a sewer, irrespective of whether they have in fact connected.

Clarifying responsibility for connections

One of the primary aims of the awareness-building campaign should be to define clearly the roles and responsibilities of the residents and the implementing agencies. For future reference and clarity, individual householders should sign written agreements which set out in simple language the responsibilities of all the parties involved. Once signed, the agreement should be considered a legal document and should be legally enforced. If possible, the agreement should be signed before construction begins, but not later than the commissioning of the scheme.

It is important that residents fully understand the implications of the document before signing which may require someone to visit each family and explain the document in detail before they sign.

Connections to rented accommodation

There is frequently controversy between landlords and tenants as to who should pay for sewer connections and the related household fittings. Where the numbers of rented accommodations are significant, local by-laws may be needed to clarify responsibility and enforce connection. Whoever is ultimately deemed responsible, it is in the implementing agency's interest to assist in any way it can to get rented accommodation connected. This may require a different regime of subsidy from that offered to owner-occupiers.

CHAPTER 6
Achieving sustainable maintenance

6.1 Responsibility for operation and maintenance

RESPONSIBILITY FOR OPERATION and maintenance is usually divided between the household and one or more institutions. The most important point is that all concerned should know unambiguously their responsibilities and duties as early in the project as possible. It is better for responsibilities to be spelled out in a formal document, signed by all interested parties, than to rely on the spoken word.

Property owners
Under normal circumstances, the householder is responsible for the operation and maintenance of all infrastructure within the plot boundary and possibly up to the junction of the house sewer and collector sewer.

Institutions
Institutions are usually responsible for all of the communal network. Where more than one institution is involved (for example where one is responsible for sewage collection and the other for sewage treatment) the most important need is to demarcate clearly areas of responsibility.

There is usually very little choice in the selection of which institutions will be involved, but it is necessary to review them to ensure that they have sufficient skills, equipment and funds to carry out their duties correctly. There may be need for institutional strengthening prior to or during the project.

Institutional responsibilities need not be carried out by the institution itself; they can be sub-contracted to private companies. Such an approach has the advantage of reducing the size of institution and reducing the cost of maintenance. This approach has worked successfully on large schemes such as Orangi in Pakistan, where the demand for routine maintenance is sufficient to support a number of private companies who compete with each other for business. On schemes where the volume of work is small, privatizing maintenance is unlikely to produce significant benefits.

There may be circumstances where institutions should be responsible for maintenance of components on private property. An obvious example would be the emptying of interceptor tanks. This is discussed in more detail in Chapter 8.

Community groups

There are a number of examples of communities being responsible for the maintenance of collector sewers, particularly where they run across household plots. Such responsibilities can be on a household basis where the plot owner is responsible for the length of sewer crossing or adjacent to his/her plot. Alternatively, a group of plot-owners may work together to maintain the collector sewer that they jointly use. It appears that joint responsibility is more appropriate to systems where the collector sewer runs under public land and individual responsibility works better where the sewer crosses the users' plots.

Attempts to make communities responsible for trunk sewers have met with little success. Most communities still feel that the removal of wastes from large groups of people should remain the responsibility of institutions.

The stability of the community has a bearing on the level of responsibility it can support. It is more difficult to enforce responsibility for maintenance in a changing population or where the sewers are installed before properties are occupied. In such areas it is more appropriate to keep consumer responsibility to within the plot boundary.

The private sector

The use of the private sector for operation and, particularly, maintenance is often overlooked but has a number of advantages. Competition for work between companies tends to reduce unit costs. The drive for larger profits speeds up work, getting jobs completed faster. The implementing agency may be able to reduce an over-inflated and under-utilized labour force resulting in savings in salaries and management. Contractors are usually less affected by political interference and union demarcations, producing a flexible and swift response to problems.

However, the use of contractors has its drawbacks as the drive for profits can lead to the use of untrained staff and the taking of short cuts, both of which can produce unsatisfactory standards of work. Contractors can use their wealth to corrupt the selection process. Contributions to politicians' re-election funds and under-paid government officials are not unknown.

Operation and maintenance using contractors must therefore be properly managed. Minimum standards of performance must be laid down and monitored. Contractor selection processes must be open to public scrutiny and seen to be fair and reasonable.

6.2 Supervision of operation and maintenance

All operation and maintenance activities must be supervised to ensure that they are carried out safely, to an approved standard, at a fair cost and within an acceptable time. Good supervision is based on a knowledge of what work must be done, why it is necessary, who is responsible for doing it and what measurable standards must be achieved. This requires the supervisors to be well-educated and trained.

Photograph 9: *Cast iron squatting plate with integral drop pipe, fitted in a toilet block with interceptor tank below. The squatting plate is removed to empty the tank.*

Photograph 10: *A well-stocked plumbing and drainage store in Pakistan, promoting private sector maintenance of the sewer network.*

Photograph 11: *A low-income housing area in Pakistan with a community constructed collector sewer. The concrete access point covers are poorly fitted, allowing silt and garbage to enter the sewer to cause maintenance problems.*

Photograph 12: *Specially shaped concrete blocks have been manufactured in Brazil to allow the construction of small diameter access chambers.*

Responsibility for supervision usually lies with the implementing agency, which is often a government agency. It is common for day-to-day activities to be contracted out to private companies. Whilst this can be much cheaper than using in-house staff, it is important that the responsible agency retains overall management control. It should set and monitor minimum standards and take responsibility for introducing new working practices when required.

Supervision of sewerage that has been implemented by community groups can be a problem. Once construction is completed, community groups often disband and leave day-to-day maintenance to individual residents. This may be satisfactory for minor problems such as local blockages, but dealing with major problems is difficult. Problems affecting a large number of properties require residents to regroup, collect funds and implement repairs. This all takes time and can create considerable social tensions. Localized maintenance by residents with no overall supervision can produce variable standards of workmanship. Residents with minimal funds available for emergencies will spend as little as possible on sewerage repair. This can lead to the long-term deterioration of the network.

In general, supervision by staff with local knowledge is an advantage. It allows for continuous contact between supervisors, the network and its users. Any problems that occur can be dealt with quickly and without the need for extensive bureaucracy. However, supervision of on-plot construction is one area where the use of local staff can be a disadvantage. Personal knowledge of the families constructing the sewers, and community pressure, may cause the supervisor to accept a standard of construction lower than that which would normally be acceptable.

Inadequate operation and maintenance is the commonest reason for sewerage schemes to fail, and persistent attention is needed to achieve long-term success. Whoever is responsible for carrying out the operation and maintenance of a scheme must be managed by an organization with the skills and legal duty to ensure that it is carried out effectively.

6.3 Minimizing maintenance: social issues

The environment in which the system is constructed and the socio-cultural attitudes of the users will have a marked effect on the type and number of operational problems that will be encountered. Some of them can be minimized by good design and construction. Others will only be reduced by re-educating the residents, and some problems cannot be prevented. A knowledge of the likely operational difficulties prior to construction will help in the project preparation and forward planning.

The following are some of the most common causes of operational difficulties produced by the environment or by the activities of residents. Measures to control the problems will bring about reductions in the cost of sewerage maintenance.

Refuse collection and disposal

Many low-income communities have no formal refuse collection system. In such cases refuse is often thrown on wasteland near or behind properties. If sewers run under such areas, the refuse can raise ground level to above the level of the access point covers, leading to ingress of silt and storm water. Vermin living off the garbage may burrow into the sewer system, particularly through poorly constructed access-point walls, leading to large volumes of silt being deposited in the sewer.

Anal cleaning practices

Communities using hard paper or solid objects for anal cleaning and disposing of the used material in the sewer are likely to experience frequent operational difficulties. The two obvious solutions are to persuade people to use soft toilet tissue or to arrange for separate disposal of the used solids.

Conversion to using soft toilet tissue can be attempted only if such tissue is easily available in the area, at an affordable price. In the short term, a maintenance organization might consider subsidizing the cost of soft toilet tissue until its use becomes commonplace.

In areas where the use of cleaning materials is common, including much of South and Central America, wastes are burned, buried or disposed of with the refuse. Of the three, immediate burning or burial are the most appropriate. The separate disposal of anal cleaning material, particularly in the domestic refuse, is not normally recommended. There are potential health and environmental hazards to residents and the refuse collectors.

Utensil washing practices

The widespread use of sand or ash for washing kitchen utensils could cause blockages in the sewerage system. However, the study upon which these guidelines are based found no evidence of this being a problem. Where sand was being used, the volume of sand discharged to the system was insignificant compared with the volume of water being used and compared with the amount of silt entering through other places, such as access points.

It is possible that the use of sand for utensil cleaning could lead to sewer blockages on very flat sites where water supply is limited, but laboratory studies indicate that this is unlikely. Should silt from utensil cleaning be considered a potential problem then the construction of silt/grease traps could be considered (see Appendix 1).

User abuse

User abuse, both deliberate and accidental, is a common cause of operational problems. Disposing of large objects such as bottles, tin cans or refuse to the sewer, making illegal connections and vandalizing access points are all relatively common. Some problems can be reduced during the design stage by selecting a minimum pipe size capable of carrying gross solids (commonly 100mm). Most, however, will only be reduced with increased consumer understanding and good system supervision.

6.4 Minimizing maintenance: system design

Surface water drainage

Sewers laid beneath or close to natural drainage channels are to be avoided. Localized changes in the channel route or bed erosion may expose the sewer, leading to infiltration of surface water and damage to the pipework and access chambers.

The use of underground junction boxes or rodding eyes instead of conventional access chambers will reduce the risk of refuse and storm water entering sewers. Wherever possible, roads above sewers should be sealed as this reduces infiltration and prevents soil erosion exposing the pipes.

Topography

Sloping sites tend to have fewer maintenance problems than flat sites. Sewers are shallower and smaller and are therefore easier to reach and cheaper to maintain. There is also less need for pumping stations which are a major source of demand for maintenance.

Water supply

All sewerage systems depend on a regular water supply. When supplies are erratic, solids build up in toilets and dry out and adhere to the invert of household drains and sewers. Such blockages may be difficult to remove when the supply is re-established.

Networks incorporating interceptor tanks are more suited to erratic water supplies. Small amounts of water can be used to flush solids into the adjoining tank where they can be stored without drying out. Sewers downstream of the tanks do not carry solids so there are no problems from the solids drying out.

Access points

Access points are a major cause of system disruption. Access covers are frequently stolen or damaged, leaving the sewer open to surface water, silt and refuse. There are a number of ways by which these problems can be minimized.

The strength of the cover will dictate the maximum load it can withstand. Lighter covers can be used in off-road situations but heavy-duty covers are needed in the public highway.

Many covers break because they are not properly located in the frame, rather than because they are of insufficient strength. This appears to be a particular problem with covers made of concrete or local stone. Although they may fit well when initially installed, poor manufacture and frame design may mean that road silt lodging on the frame rim prevents proper relocation once they have been removed. Attention to detailed design and construction of the cover and rim will reduce this problem.

In some communities, access covers have a resale value either for recycling or for using on another site. This is particularly true of metal covers. Fitting the cover with a locking mechanism may reduce the problem but it may be necessary to switch to a cover made of a material with a lower resale value (e.g. concrete or stone).

Measures which reduce capital cost such as extending the spacing of access points and replacing them with underground buried access chambers or rodding eyes (Chapter 4) will reduce maintenance costs by removing or reducing the number of places susceptible to abuse.

Trunk sewers and pumping stations

Trunk sewers do not normally require much maintenance but when they do, the disruption caused can be considerable. Maintenance is more essential for pumping stations, which require regular attention to prevent breakdown. Local micro-drainage systems (Chapter 4) will minimize the number of trunk sewers and pumping stations.

Sewage treatment

Localized drainage networks will increase the number of treatment plants required and this will increase the maintenance requirements of the system. In general, small treatment plants utilize lower levels of technology than large plants. Therefore, in areas where skilled manpower is in short supply or where spare parts for electromechanical equipment are difficult to obtain, small treatment plants are more appropriate than large ones.

Interceptor tanks

If interceptor tanks are not emptied on a regular basis, they will fill with solids which will then overflow into the sewer network, causing maintenance problems downstream. The main problem is that whilst interceptor tanks are usually on private property and privately owned, infrequent emptying will create difficulties in the communally owned part of the network. Furthermore, tank-emptying is an activity requiring trained staff and specialist equipment. Experience in Nigeria and Zambia has shown that if it is left to individual residents, it may be ignored or done so badly as to cause serious environmental and health hazards (Vines 1991).

It would seem logical that the organization that benefits from having the tanks emptied should organize it, so the organization responsible for the maintenance of the communal network should take responsibility. In many communities the entry of strangers onto private property would be strongly resisted. Locating interceptor tanks near the property boundary with access directly to the road may be a solution. Alternatively, it may be necessary to enact local by-laws giving right of entry for tank-emptying personnel. Such an approach will only work if the community gives its support to the by-law's enactment.

6.5 Construction quality

Many of the maintenance problems associated with sewers are caused during construction either by the use of inappropriate materials or poor supervision. Some of the most common problems are mentioned below.

Supervision

Poor supervision is one of the most common reasons for poor construction. This is because contractors may take advantage of poor supervision and use inappropriate materials or construction methods to save cost. It may also be because the contractors lack the necessary skills to carry out the work correctly without the advice of a qualified supervisor.

Good supervision requires that skilled staff pay frequent visits to well-designed projects let under clearly defined contracts. Normally this requires the services of engineers or technicians from the implementing agency. Alternatively, local residents can take on the supervision. This has proved successful for the supervision of simple structures such as collector sewers, provided appropriate training is given.

Such an approach has numerous advantages. Under-staffed implementing agencies can manage large numbers of small contracts at the same time. Local residents will have a direct interest in the sewers being laid and are therefore likely to take a keen interest in the quality of their construction. This interest can be further fostered if the residents have made a financial contribution to the project.

Construction components

The decision as to what quality of components to use for a project is always a compromise between the capital cost and the future cost of maintenance. The components of most importance are pipes, pipe joints and access chambers. All are discussed in more detail in Chapter 4.

On-plot construction

The projects upon which these guidelines are based highlighted poor on-plot construction as one of the main causes of operational difficulties. Traditionally, construction within the plot boundary has been considered the sole responsibility of the resident. Shortages of money and poor construction skills have led to many household sewerage systems being the primary source of ingress of silt and storm water. Only close supervision of on-plot construction by the operating agency will prevent this occurring.

Photograph 13: *Laying a house connection from a condominial sewer in a low-income housing area in north-east Brazil.*

CHAPTER 7
Optimizing the return on investment in sewerage

AN INSTITUTION WISHING to implement an on-going and sustainable sewerage programme must aim to recoup all or part of its investment. It may be possible to rely on government subsidies and grants to cover capital investment but it should never be relied on to cover operational expenses. Government priorities change and political expediency and macro-economics may lead to rapid changes in investment policies. Institutions that have relied on government support have frequently found their funding cut off or curtailed at short notice. Community-based funding, if properly managed, is much more reliable. Furthermore, payment instils a feeling of ownership in the services provided and reduces abuse. The aim should always be to install sewerage schemes that are affordable by the recipient communities so that repayment can be guaranteed. At the very least, communities should be expected to pay for the operational costs. This chapter will examine ways of maximizing a community's contribution to the capital investment and operational costs.

7.1 Tariffs
The regular collection of a charge for the services supplied is probably the commonest method of recouping investment and operational costs. Tariffs are flexible and can be altered in line with inflation and to reflect changes in costs. They can reflect people's ability to pay and can be used for cross-subsidy between rich and poor communities.

Setting an appropriate tariff is irrelevant if the tariff is not collected or amended to reflect changes in costs. Many of the sewerage schemes visited during the preparation of these guidelines were suffering from inadequate funding because tariffs were not being collected or because the tariff had not been increased in line with inflation. The latter was a particular problem in Brazil, where annual inflation was extremely high.

The commonest (probably the most effective) method of collecting sewerage charges is to collect the tariff along with that of another utility, usually water. Such an approach saves on collection costs and provides a method for punishing non-payers: disconnecting the water supply. Where water supplies are metered, it has the additional benefit of charging people in line with the amount of use they make of the system. Difficulties often occur when water and sewerage are managed by different organizations or the tariff is collected by a third party (often the local council). Tariffs may be withheld because of the non-payment of debts incurred by other sections of the sewage agency.

Adding the cost of sewerage to a local housing tax, or collecting the sum as part of a local income tax have been suggested, but little information exists on the effectiveness of such approaches.

When the residents are directly responsible for a major proportion of the operation and maintenance of a sewerage system, the tariff needed to cover the provision for other parts of the system may be so low as to make the collection of an individual tariff uneconomic. It may be more appropriate to collect the tariff communally. One member of the community collects the tariff from the local residents and pays it in a lump sum to the institution. Such an approach only works where there is trust between residents but it does give them an opportunity to subsidize poor members of the community.

7.2 Direct repayment of capital costs

A number of communities in Brazil and Pakistan have only been able to obtain a sewerage system if the residents have contributed directly to the cost of the sewer network, particularly the collector sewers. Some communities have only been able to afford it by collecting the money incrementally. Paying connection costs incrementally either before or after construction allows the cost to be spread over a longer period, making payment easier.

Payment in advance reduces the capital investment required from the implementing agency. Problems may arise if there is a long delay between residents making their payments and the work commencing.

Retrospective payment puts more responsibility on the implementing agency to collect loans, as failure to do so will increase their overall investment. If schemes are to be self-financing, loan repayments must reflect the real value of the investment, including local inflation rates.

Consideration must be given to the repayment period. Short repayment periods will mean large payment increments whilst long repayment periods will increase overall institutional costs, tie up more capital and be more difficult to collect as residents quickly 'forget' the benefits gained by sewerage and thus lose interest in repaying loans. If repayment must be long term, it is better to include it in the sewerage tariff rather than collect it separately. In general, loan repayment rates should be set as high as possible, with perhaps differential repayment rates for different income levels. Where differential repayment rates are used, the criteria for selection must be defined and understood by the community so that there is no feeling that some families are receiving preferential treatment.

7.3 Minimizing tariffs and maximizing returns

Minimizing the cost of operation and maintenance will reduce unit costs and hence tariffs. Lower tariffs will encourage connections and thus increase returns. One way to reduce costs is to transfer some of the operation and maintenance responsibilities to the community. They are the ones who will suffer from poor maintenance and so they are more likely to deal with any problems quickly. Community-based maintenance is discussed in more detail in Chapter 6.

It is an unfortunate fact of life that implementing agencies often have their financial plans thwarted by political interference. Rapidly rising tariffs with no perceptible improvements in service are often seen by local politicians as a barrier to their re-election and are therefore resisted. The economic realities of recent years have led many politicians to see the benefits of privatization. Although privatization gives an institution the flexibility to introduce hard economic approaches to service provision, it also removes its access to subsidies.

If privatization is unacceptable then political support for schemes is crucial if repayment is to be maintained. This is particularly important where countries have high inflation rates and political support is required to increase repayment rates. At times of poor economic growth, high inflation or high unemployment, politicians may be understandably unwilling to sanction something that will increase the financial burden being placed on the poor.

Photograph 14: *Constructing an underground junction box in Sao Paulo, Brazil. Compare this with a conventional access chamber shown in Figure A1.1.*

CHAPTER 8
Non-conventional sewerage systems

THE MEASURES DISCUSSED in the previous two chapters can be combined in various combinations to suit local circumstances. In the past these combinations have produced three broad sewerage groups. They are:

○ Simplified sewerage
○ Condominial sewerage
○ Interceptor tank systems.

These names are by no means universal: interceptor tank systems are sometimes called 'small-bore sewerage'; condominial sewerage is often described as 'shallow sewerage' or 'back-service connections'. The names describe general scheme types. Within each, a wide range of technologies and approaches are employed. There are also numerous areas of commonality.

8.1 Simplified sewerage

Simplified sewerage examines conventional sewerage design and construction practices and adjusts them to reflect the environment and affordability of recipient communities. In most cases this produces a reduction in cost but there is also some easing of institutional responsibility. The system has been widely adopted in Brazil where over fifty systems have been installed in Sao Paulo State alone (Azavedo Netto 1989). Many of the concepts have been incorporated in the Brazilian codes for sewerage and drainage (MDU/PNUD 1986).

The construction costs of simplified sewerage have been reduced by means of the following design features. All are discussed in detail in Chapter 4.

○ Reducing the minimum pipe size for collector sewers to 100mm.
○ Reducing the minimum collector sewer gradients to 1 : 220 or less.
○ Replacing conventional access points with ones of smaller diameter or with rodding eyes or underground chambers.
○ Increasing the spacing between access points.
○ Postponing the construction of treatment plants.

A comparison of the costs of simplified sewerage and conventional sewerage in Sao Paulo State are shown in Table 8.1.

Table 8.1: Comparison of the construction costs of simplified and conventional sewerage in Sao Paulo State, Brazil

Item	Cost of simplified sewerage (US$ in 1988) per connection	Cost of conventional sewerage (US$ in 1988) per connection
House sewers	110 – 220	110 – 220
Collector and trunk sewers	550 – 880	1100 – 1650
Treatment plant	110 – 220	165 – 275
Total	770 – 1320	1375 – 2145

Note: Costs assume an average of 5.5 people per connection

Source: Adapted from Azavedo Netto (1989)

8.2 Condominial sewerage

Condominial sewerage is typified by the laying of the collector sewers at the rear of properties, close to the point of waste generation. A typical layout is shown in Figure 8.1. It is currently being implemented in a number of states in north-east Brazil but it was used widely in the UK during the middle of the 19th century (Latham 1878).

Construction costs have been reduced by:

○ Adopting a back-service collector sewer layout, thus reducing the length of house sewers and minimizing the sewer depth.
○ Constructing localized systems so as to minimize pumping stations and trunk sewers.
○ Making use of under-utilized municipal resources during construction.

Institutional costs have been reduced by transferring responsibility for maintenance of the collector sewers constructed on-plot to the block residents.

Some municipalities have promoted implementation by insisting on a block being fully sewered before surfacing the adjoining roads.

Condominial sewerage lends itself to direct community funding. The number of families living in a housing block is small enough for them to work and plan together. As with other community-based projects there is evidence of some members of the block being pressured into participating, but there is also evidence of informal cross-subsidy between the rich and poor of the block.

A number of authors have compared the cost of condominial sewerage with that of conventional sewerage and on-site sanitation. As would be expected, differences vary, but in general, condominial sewerage is about half the cost of conventional sewerage and one and a half to two times the cost of on-site sanitation (Vines 1991).

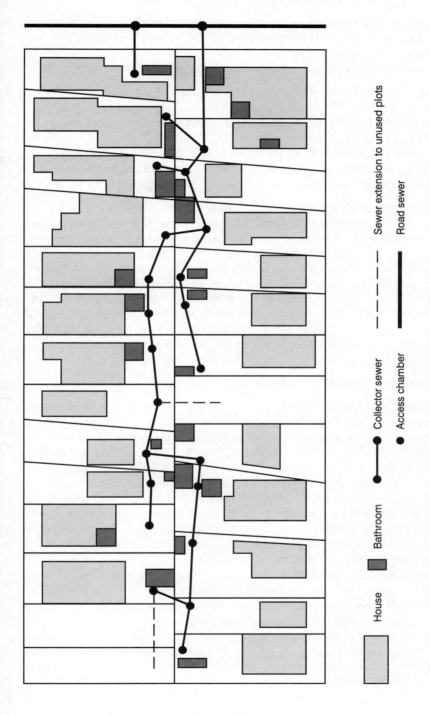

House **Bathroom**   **Collector sewer**   **Sewer extension to unused plots**

Access chamber   **Road sewer**

Figure 8.1 *Condominial sewer layout in Petrolina, Brazil*

Once constructed, condominial sewerage appears to function satisfactorily. The main problems relate to slow implementation, low connection rates and poor cost recoupment.

Slow construction and low connection rates have been caused by:

○ Poor community motivation and mobilization.
○ Under-staffing.
○ Vandalism by residents opposed to the system. (Some consider the system inferior to conventional sewerage.)
○ Implementation by institutions with little experience of sewerage.
○ Residents unable to fund the construction of house sewers.
○ Project areas where no established community organizations exist.

Many unplanned settlements have developed with dwellings built haphazardly and close together without proper access. Constructing sewerage of any type in such situations would almost certainly entail some redevelopment with its consequential social and economic implications.

It is not clear if the condominial system could be extended to new housing developments. The capital cost could be reclaimed as part of the general loan repayment but there is no way of knowing in advance whether individuals would be willing to undertake sewer maintenance. There are many communal sewers in the UK and there does not appear to be a problem with their maintenance provided it forms part of the land purchase agreement.

8.3 Interceptor tank systems

Interceptor tank systems have been constructed in many parts of the world including Australia, Brazil, Nigeria, Pakistan and Zambia. They vary considerably in design and construction but all rely on some form of settlement tank close to the house to remove some or all of the suspended solids in the effluent and to dampen peak flows (see Chapter 4). This allows the design of the downstream sewer network to be relaxed, producing savings in capital and operating costs. Some schemes, such as the one in Brotas, Brazil (Figure 8.2) have been designed specifically to include interceptor tanks whereas others, such as those in Australia, have been developed to collect the effluent from existing septic tanks in areas where conventional drainage fields have failed or potable groundwater sources are being polluted.

Experience has shown that large interceptor tanks (see Chapter 4 for definition), which have been properly designed, constructed, and maintained, will support sewer networks laid at very flat gradients and with peak design velocities of less than 0.05m/s. In addition, the damping effect of interceptor tanks on peak flows and their removal of gross solids allow for the satisfactory use of sewer pipes as small as 40mm diameter and perhaps less. Furthermore, large interceptor tanks will reduce the amount of treatment required at the point of final discharge (Vines 1991). However, the effluent

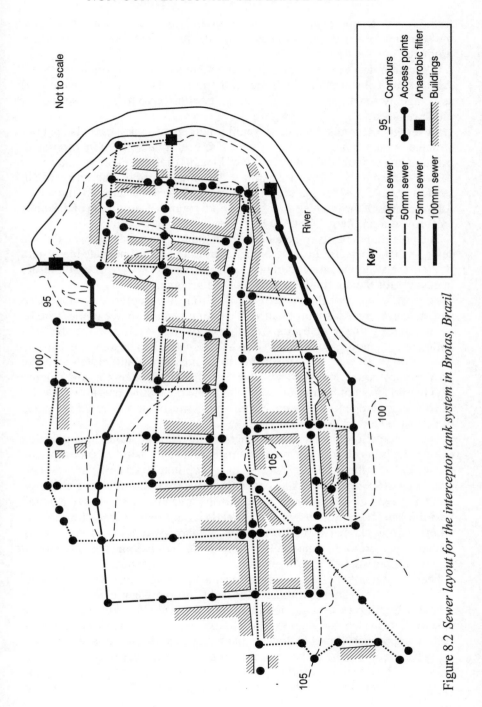

Figure 8.2 *Sewer layout for the interceptor tank system in Brotas, Brazil*

from large interceptor tanks will almost certainly be anaerobic and this limits the selection of sewer pipes to those manufactured from non-cementacious products.

Interceptor tanks have the potential for making sewerage work at lower per capita water consumption levels than those required to support conventional sewerage systems, since the distance that solids have to be transported is much reduced.

Sewerage networks including small interceptor tanks have been constructed in Pakistan and Zambia. These interceptor tanks were incorporated, presumably, to reduce the possibility of blockages in the downstream sewer network in an area of low per capita water consumption. The downstream sewer network was designed using conventional criteria with no allowance for the effects of the interceptor tanks. In both countries, emptying of the tanks has proved a problem (Vines 1991).

The potential benefits to be gained from interceptor tanks with small bore sewers will be lost if future developments are allowed to connect to the system without constructing interceptor tanks. Strong planning controls are therefore necessary for the continuing success of the scheme.

The collection and disposal of sludge from interceptor tanks has been shown to be a significant problem with existing systems. None of the systems visited during the preparation for this book had facilities for the safe collection of sludge. No consideration had been given to its ultimate disposal (Reed 1993). Designers of a scheme in Brotas, Brazil attempted to make provision by constructing a drying bed next to each interceptor tank (Figure 8.3) but this has not been a success. The high water-table prevailing locally prevents the sludge from drying. No provision was made for the safe disposal of the dried sludge.

The principal problems related to desludging revolve around the question of responsibility. Under normal circumstances, responsibility for emptying would lie with the property owners since the interceptor tanks are on their properties. Residents who are not owners have no incentive to desludge regularly. Desludging costs money and is inconvenient, and silt overflowing into the sewerage system will not directly affect them but will affect the communal sewer network downstream. If the sewer system is to work effectively, therefore, responsibility for tank desludging must devolve to the organization responsible for communal sewer maintenance.

There are a number of ways of ensuring that tanks are emptied satisfactorily. In Australia, for example, interceptor tanks are regularly inspected by the municipal authorities. Legal and institutional powers have been enacted to ensure that householders empty their tanks when requested (Vines 1991). Another approach would be for the maintenance authority to take responsibility for emptying the tanks and then to charge the residents for the service. This could be either a one-off payment or included in the general tariff. Both approaches would require the right of municipal authorities to enter proper-

Photograph 15: *Double toilet block, Zambia. Each toilet discharges to an interceptor tank below and then to a collector sewer. Note the poor standard of repair. Householders pay no tariff and the local authority has little money for maintenance.*

Photograph 16: *Four-unit toilet block discharging to a communal interceptor tank, Nigeria. The access is in the centre of the picture.*

Photograph 17: *Asbestos-cement squatting plate, Nigeria.*

Photograph 18: *Demonstration two-chamber interceptor tank on a small bore sewerage system, Brazil. In the foreground is the inlet from the house. The chamber to the left is to receive sludge from the interceptor tank where it is allowed to dry before removal.*

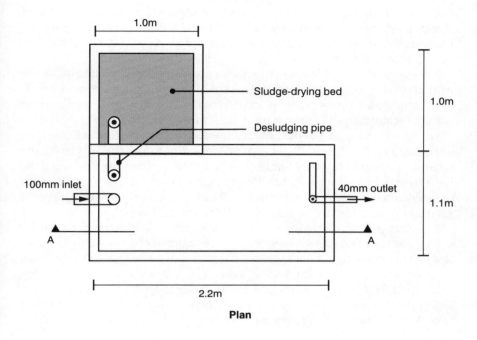

Plan

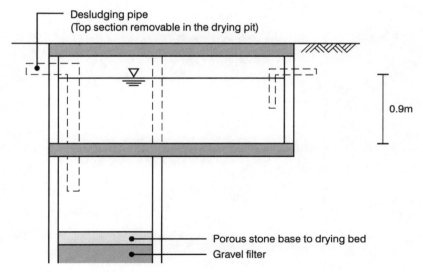

Section through A-A

Figure 8.3 *On-plot interceptor tank with sludge-drying bed, Brotas, Brazil (as shown in Photograph 18, opposite)*

ties without the permission of the property owner. There are a number of societies where this would be unacceptable on social or religious grounds. Constructing interceptor tanks on or near the property boundary, so that they can be accessed from the public highway, may be a solution.

Provision of sludge disposal facilities must probably remain with the institution responsible for the maintenance of the communal sewer network. The commonest options are to incorporate the sludge with sludge from sewage treatment plants or to bury it in a sanitary landfill.

The construction cost of the sewered interceptor tank system in Brotas has been calculated as being 78 per cent cheaper than a conventional sewerage scheme in a nearby town of similar size. Schemes in South Australia and the USA have shown savings of 25 to 35 per cent but this usually excludes the cost of the interceptor tanks. Data from the USA also tentatively shows significant savings in operation and maintenance (Vines et al. 1989).

There is evidence that sewered, large interceptor tank systems can produce considerable capital cost savings. Savings are more likely on schemes serving low density populations where reductions in cost of pipework are greater than the additional cost of the interceptor tanks. The provision of adequate sludge removal and disposal facilities may significantly reduce this cost advantage. Only a careful financial evaluation of the capital and operational costs of each scheme will determine whether an interceptor tank system is appropriate.

APPENDIX 1
Glossary of terms

Access points
Points of entry into the sewer network for observation and maintenance. They are usually large enough to allow the entry of a person or persons (Figure A1.1). They are located at sewer intersections, changes in sewer direction, gradient or size and at a spacing dictated by the methods of sewer cleaning being used.

Access point on the highway boundary
The same as any other property access point, located on the property and adjacent to the highway boundary. It is used for observation and maintenance of the sewer and also marks the change of responsibility. Upstream it is the responsibility of the property-owner whilst downstream it is the responsibility of the authority in charge of maintenance of the communal sewerage network.

Branch drains
Pipes connected to the waste outlet of water-using appliances such as WCs and wash-basins after the water-trap. As such they usually run above ground. The design of branch drains is not covered by this book; readers are referred to BS 8301 (1987) for further details.

Collector sewer
Collects effluent from properties and other waste-producing sources (such as industries) and carries them by gravity and in increasing volume to the discharge point. They are commonly constructed under public highways so as to be accessible to properties on both sides of the road and easy to reach for maintenance.

Grease trap
A small underground tank attached to a house sewer. It is designed to collect excess grease and/or sand and prevents them precipitating in the nearby sewer network and causing blockages. (Sand is used for washing pots and pans.)

Gully trap
Gully traps are installed where branch drains enter house sewers. They allow the entry of sullage into the house sewers whilst preventing the escape of foul sewer gases.

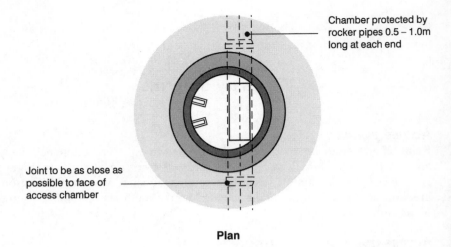

Plan

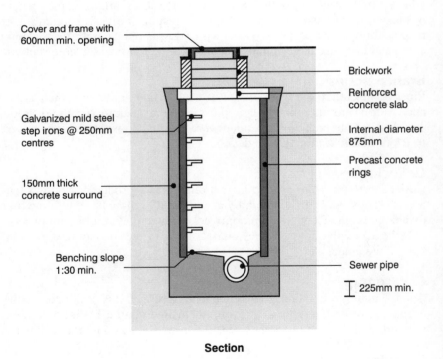

Section

Figure A1.1 *Detail of a typical access chamber for a sewer 1.35 – 3.0m deep*
Source: *Adapted from WAA (1989)*

House sewer (or house drain)

Collects wastes discharged from individual or groups of sanitary fittings via the branch drains inside a building. The house sewer is nearly always below ground.

Interceptor tanks

Underground storage tanks set in the line of the house sewer, usually near the highway boundary, designed to reduce the amount of solids in the sewer network. Small tanks have a liquid volume of around 250 litres and provide 4 to 6 hours' retention, while large tanks provide approximately 24 hours' storage.

Property access point

A hole over the house sewer which gives access for observation and maintenance. Access points are commonly provided wherever the house sewer changes direction, slope or size and at sewer intersections.

Trunk sewer

A sewer receiving effluent from a number of collector sewers and carrying sewage in bulk from one point to another. It usually receives very little effluent directly from individual properties.

Ventilation pipe

A vertical pipe extending from the house sewer to a point above the highest opening in the property. The pipe is open at the top and allows the escape of the foul gases produced in the sewer system to be discharged into the atmosphere without causing annoyance to residents. The ventilation pipe also conveys wastes from upper floors to the house sewer.

APPENDIX 2
The design of interceptor tanks

Principles of tank design

It is recommended that large interceptor tanks be designed using the same principles as those applied to septic tanks. The guidelines for interceptor tanks given below are based on those given for septic tanks in Franceys et al. 1992.

The guiding principles of tank design are:

○ to provide sufficient retention time for sewage in the tank, thus allowing separation of solids and stabilization of the liquid;
○ to provide stable quiescent hydraulic conditions for efficient settlement and flotation of solids;
○ to ensure that the tank is large enough to store accumulated sludge and scum;
○ to ensure that no blockages are likely to occur;
○ to ensure that there is adequate ventilation, thus preventing the possibility of a build-up of explosive or corrosive gases.

The removal efficiency of solids can be as high as 80 per cent but it depends on retention time, inlet and outlet arrangements, and frequency of desludging.

Sludge and scum generation

Organic matter in the sewage either settles to the bottom of the tank or rises to the liquid surface depending on its relative density to water. The organic matter is broken down by anaerobic bacteria, reducing it to gases, liquids and a residual solid. The rate of digestion is temperature-dependent, being greatest at 35°C.

The scum layer is made up of grease, oil and other floating matter. It can become quite hard. The sewage flows through the tank, sandwiched between the scum and the sludge.

The sludge on the tank floor is compressed by the water and by the accumulated sludge above. Hence the volume of sludge is considerably less than that of the raw sewage solids.

Calculating tank volume

Liquid volume

The tank has to be large enough to allow quiescent conditions to develop for long enough for the maximum amount of solids to settle out of suspension. For domestic applications a retention time of 24 hours' is normally necessary but as the flow increases, conditions within the tank become less turbulent allowing smaller retention times to be used. The following retention times are recommended:

If Q is less than 6   T = 24
If Q is between 6 and 14   T = 33 − 1.5Q
If Q is greater than 14   T = 12

where Q is the daily wastewater flow rate in cubic metres per day and T is the liquid retention time in hours.

Wastewater flow rates are usually considered as 90 per cent of water consumption up to a maximum water consumption of 250 litres per person. Above this figure it is assumed the water is being used for garden watering, car washing and so on.

The tank volume required for liquid $(A) = Q \times T \div 24$.

Sludge and scum volume

The volume required for sludge and scum accumulation can be calculated from the formula:

$$B = P \times N \times F \times S$$

where

B is the required sludge and scum storage volume
P is the number of people using the tank
N is the number of years between desludging (normally 2 − 5 years)
F is a factor which relates sludge digestion rate to temperature and desludging intervals as shown in table A2.1.
S is the rate of sludge and scum accumulation. The figure should be determined locally but if that is not possible it can be assumed to be 25 litres per person per year for WC wastes only and 40 litres per person per year for WC and sullage wastes.

Table A2.1: Value of the sizing factor 'F' for calculating sludge and scum accumulation

Number of years between desludging	Value of 'F' Ambient temperature		
	> 20°C throughout the year	> 10°C throughout the year	< 10°C throughout the year
1	1.3	1.5	2.5
2	1.0	1.15	1.5
3	1.0	1.0	1.27
4	1.0	1.0	1.15
5	1.0	1.0	1.06
6 or more	1.0	1.0	1.0

Total tank volume

Total tank volume (C) = A + B.

In practice it is not recommended to construct tanks having a volume less than one cubic metre.

Tank shape and dimensions

The following guidelines can be used for determining the internal dimensions of a rectangular tank.

The invert of the outlet pipe (and hence the liquid level) should be at least 1.2m above the tank floor. 1.5m is preferable. The depth of the tank should be less than the total length. In addition, a clear space of 0.3m should be left between the liquid level and the under surface of the tank cover.

The width of the tank should be at least 0.6m to allow entry for construction and maintenance.

The tank should be divided into two compartments with the first compartment twice the size of the second. (For a tank of width 'W' the length of the first tank should be '2W' and the second tank 'W'.)

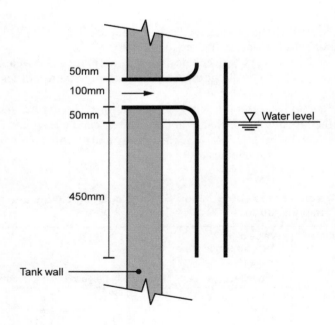

Figure A2.1 *Tank inlet pipe*

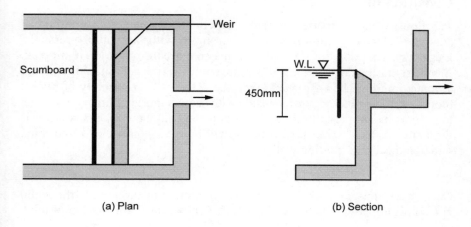

(a) Plan　　　　　　　　　　　(b) Section

Figure A2.2 *Tank outlet using overflow weir*

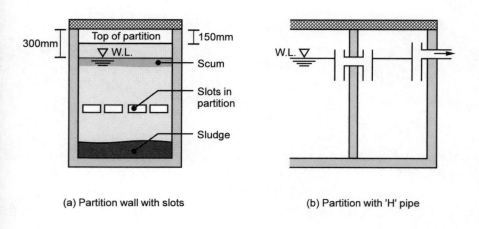

(a) Partition wall with slots　　　　　　(b) Partition with 'H' pipe

Figure A2.3 *Options for flow-through tank partitions*

Construction

The floors of small household tanks are commonly made of unreinforced concrete 0.1 – 0.15m thick, which is strong to withstand uplift pressures. Larger tanks or poor ground conditions may require the base to be reinforced. The floor may be flat or sloping. If sloping, only the first tank should slope and at a maximum of 1 in 4 towards the inlet. The walls are usually of bricks, blocks or stone, rendered on the inside with cement mortar. Larger communal tanks must be properly designed by a competent engineer. The tank cover is normally made of reinforced concrete with access points above the inlet, outlet and central dividing wall.

Inlet
The sewage must enter the tank with a minimum of disturbance to the liquid and solids already in the tank. Figure A2.1 shows a suitable design of inlet.

Outlet
For tanks less than 1.2m wide, a simple 'T' pipe arrangement similar to the inlet can be used. Tanks wider than 1.2m should have a full width weir protected by a scum board (Figure A2.2).

Dividing wall
Flow between the two compartments can be controlled by either slots in the dividing wall or an 'H' pipe as shown in Figure A2.3.

REFERENCES

These guidelines are based on two research projects undertaken by the author and funded by the Overseas Development Administration of the United Kingdom. The first project reviewed the literature published about ways of reducing the cost of sewerage (Vines, Reed & Pickford 1989). The second project evaluated a number of existing reduced-cost sewerage schemes that have been constructed in various developing countries. It also conducted laboratory experiments to investigate the movement of solids in the upper regions of sewerage systems. Individual reports were prepared for each of the systems evaluated and for the laboratory research. These reports are fully referenced here and their results are summarized in Reed (1993). Other parts of the book draw on the author's personal experience of low-cost sewerage and on-site sanitation in many parts of the world.

Azavedo Netto, J.M. 1989. 'Innovative and low-cost technologies utilized in sewerage – final draft'. Report prepared for the Pan American Health Organization (PAHO), Lima, Peru.

Bartlett, R.E. 1970. *Public Health Engineering Design in Metric: Sewerage*. Elsevier Publishing, Barking, UK.

British Standards Institute (BS) 8005. 1987. 'British Standard Sewerage – Part 1. Guide to new sewerage construction'. UK.

British Standards Institute (BS) 8301. 1985. 'British Standard Code of Practice for Building Drainage'. UK.

Franceys R., Pickford J., Reed R. 1992. *A Guide to the Development of On-site Sanitation*. World Health Organisation, Geneva, Switzerland. ISBN 92 4 154443 0.

Kalbermatten, J.M., Julius, D.S., Gunnerson, C.G. 1982.*Appropriate sanitation alternatives: a technical and economic appraisal*. John Hopkins University Press, Baltimore, USA.

Latham, B. 1878. *Sanitary Engineering*. Spon, London, UK.

Ministerio do Desenvolviomento Urbano e Meio Ambiente and Programa das Nacoes Unidas para o Desenvolviomento (MDU/PNUD). 1986. *Redes de esgote simplificadas: manual tecnico 1*. Ministerio do Desenvolviomento Urbano e Meio Ambiente, Brasilia.

Orangi Pilot Project (OPP) 1989. 'Low-cost sanitation programme of the Orangi Pilot Project Research and Training Institute: Statistical data (survey November 1989)' Karachi, Pakistan.

Reed R. 1993. 'Reduced Cost Sewerage in Developing Countries: Phase Two – Final Report'. WEDC, Loughborough University of Technology, UK.

Severn Trent Water International (STI). 1993. 'The Sewerage Masterplan for the Islands of Mauritius and Rodrigues – Development Programme – Rural Areas, Final Report'. Prepared for Min. Energy, Water Resources and Postal Service. Govt of Mauritius.

Standards Association of Australia (AS) 1990. 'National plumbing and drainage code. Part 2: Sanitary plumbing and sanitary drainage'. Standard Australia, Sydney, Australia.

Tucker C., Kimber J. 1994. 'Rural Sewage Pollution in the '90s'. Report of the rural sewerage project 1993/94. National Rivers Authority, Lower Severn Area, Tewkesbury, UK.

United Nations Centre for Human Settlements (Habitat) 1986. *The Design of Shallow Sewers*. Nairobi, Kenya. ISBN 92 1 131019 9.

Vines M. 1991. *Non Conventional Sewerage in Developing Countries*. Masters Thesis submitted to Loughborough University of Technology, UK.

Vines M., Reed R., Pickford J. 1989. *Reduced Cost Sewerage for Developing Countries*. WEDC, Loughborough University of Technology, UK.

Water Authorities Association (WAA) 1989. 'Sewers for adoption – A design and construction guide for developers', 3rd edition. Water Research Centre, UK.

Wiseman, R., 1988. 'Latin crisis needs political priority'. *World Water,* 11, No 10, pp. 15-17.

World Bank 1991. 'Environmental assessment source book – Volume II – Sectoral guidelines'. Technical paper No. 140. IBRD, Washington D.C., USA.

FURTHER READING

In addition to the references, the following publications are recommended for readers who would like further information on the design and construction of conventional and reduced-cost sewerage systems. *It does not include publications specifically covering sewage treatment.*

Bakalian A., Wright A., Otis R., Netto, J. Azavedo. 1994. *Simplified Sewerage: Design Guidelines*. Water and Sanitation Report 7. UNDP-World Bank Water and Sanitation Program, Washington, USA.

Institute of Plumbing 1988. *Plumbing Engineering Services Design Guide*. UK.

McNab A., Reed R. 1991. *Laboratory investigation of the movement of solids in shallow gradient sewers with low flush volumes*. WEDC, Loughborough University of Technology, UK.

Netto, Jose M. Azavedo, 1992. *Innovative and Low-Cost Technologies Utilized in Sewerage.* Technical Series No. 29. World Health Organization. Washington D.C., USA.

Otis R.J., Mara D.D. 1985. *The Design of Small Bore Sewer Systems.* UNDP. TAG Technical Note No. 14. World Bank, Washington, USA.

Reed R., Vines M. 1992. *Sewered aqua privies in New Bussa, Kwara State, Nigeria.* WEDC, Loughborough University of Technology, UK.

Reed R., Vines M. 1992. *Reduced cost sewerage in Avai, Sao Paulo State, Brazil.* WEDC, Loughborough University of Technology, UK.

Reed R., Vines M. 1992. *Condominial Sewerage in Petrolina and other towns in Pernambuco State, Brazil.* WEDC, Loughborough University of Technology, UK.

Reed R., Vines M. 1992. *Condominial sewerage in Basin 'E', Natal, Rio Grande Do Norte, Brazil.* WEDC, Loughborough University of Technology, UK.

Reed R., Vines M. 1992. *Sewered interceptor tank systems in Brotas, Ceara State, Brazil.* WEDC, Loughborough University of Technology, UK.

Reed R., Vines M. 1992. *Reduced cost sewerage in Orangi, Karachi, Pakistan.* WEDC, Loughborough University of Technology, UK.

Reed R., Vines M. 1992. *Reduced cost sewerage in the community development project, Orangi, Karachi, Pakistan.* WEDC, Loughborough University of Technology, UK.

Vines M., Reed R.1991. *Evaluation of sewered aqua privies in Matero, Lusaka, Zambia.* WEDC, Loughborough University of Technology, UK.

Vines M., Reed R.1991. *Evaluation of sewered aqua privies in Kabushi, Ndola, Zambia.* WEDC, Loughborough University of Technology, UK.

Tayler K., Cotton A. 1993. *Urban Upgrading – Options and procedures for Pakistan.* WEDC, Loughborough University of Technology, UK.

INDEX

About the author
Bob Reed is a Programme and Project Manager at the Water, Engineering and Development Centre, UK. He specializes in water supply and sanitation for rural areas, low-income urban communities and refugees. He has considerable experience of training, design and project implementation in the Pacific, the Caribbean, Asia and Africa. In recent years he has focused on the problems of upgrading water and sanitation services to the urban poor at a price they can afford.